DEVELOPMENTAL PSYCHOLOGY
A GUIDE TO DEVELOPMENTAL AND CHILD PSYCHOLOGY
THIRD EDITION

CONNOR WHITELEY

INTRODUCTION
As always I hate introductions.

Especially, if they are long and boring but like this book, my introduction will not be long and boring.

So in this book, I will explain what developmental psychology is and the various ways how our development impacts our behaviour. From the attachments we form to the impacts that our peers have on us in the present and future and a lot more.

However, almost everything in this book is explained in an engaging and easy to understand way, because I hate standard psychology books with their boring tone.

Therefore, this book will be different but still deliver great information about Developmental Psychology.

Who Is This Book For?

In short, this book is for anyone interested in psychology or social sciences and they want to learn about child development as well as how our development impacts our behaviour.

Who Am I?

Personally, I always like to know about the author of a nonfiction book, so I know that they're qualified to talk about the topic.

So in case you're like me, I am Connor Whiteley a psychology author of over 10 psychology books, I run a psychology blog at www.connorwhiteley.net, I'm the host of The Psychology World Podcast and I'm a psychology student at the University of Kent in England.

So now that we have everything out the way, let's start learning about developmental psychology...

CHAPTER 1: INTRODUCTION TO DEVELOPMENTAL PSYCHOLOGY AND MORDERN THEORIES

So we know that Developmental Psychology is about studying children, but why study children and their development instead of something else? Like: mental conditions.

Well, studying children helps us to understand how adults are structured and we study their development because you are very different from the person you were at 5 years old.

Also, developmental psychology never ends as it focuses on development throughout the human lifespan.

What is Developmental Psychology?

Developmental psychology is a serious theoretical science contributing to the discussion of how the human mind is internally organised.

(Karmiloff, 1992, p.13) and developmental psychology isn't merely a cute empirical database when a behaviour can be observed.

Reason being that developmental psychology can give us clues to how an adult's cognition is structured.

In other words, if we can understand how prejudice, racism and more develop in childhood then we can understand it more in adults.

Fundamental Questions in Developmental Psychology:

Within this subfield of psychology, there are a lot of fundamental questions about our existence that it aims to answer.

For example:

- Why am I the way I am?
- What do you start with?
- How does it change?

Time Periods:

When I first started developmental psychology, I was very relieved that our brilliant lecturer defined to us the different stages of development. As I knew the university and other psychology professionals are very strict and get annoyed if you mix up the terms of child development.

You can see the stages of child development below:

- Prenatal conception-born
- Infancy/toddlerhood birth- 2 years
- Early childhood 2-6 years
- Middle childhood 6-11
- Adolescents 12-18 years
- Early adulthood 18-25 years

What's a Developmental Theory?

Like anything in psychology, we need a theory to be able to explain why something happens and in developmental psychology, we need our theories to explain how a child develops.

In addition, developmental theories need to describe and explain behaviour as well as they can use the following questions as guidance:

- What's the beginning state of the behaviour?
- What changes over time?
- Why/ how do these changes happen?

Even with these questions as guidance, how do you know where to start?

Therefore, there are a few different starting points that developmental psychologists can take.

For example, they could start off with the

Empiricist idea that humans are blank slates that learn overtime as well as; using a technology reference; humans come with very little software uploaded.

Or they could believe in the Nativist idea that humans come preloaded with all the information that they need as everything is predetermined by our genes and biology.

Changes Over Time:

Therefore, using these two ideas how do they explain how humans change and learn as they grow older?

According to the blank slate idea, we learn the structure of knowledge that is organised into cognitive structures.

In other words, we develop because of our experiences and we learn things about the world, but the mechanism behind our learning differs by theory.

On the other hand, the Nativist idea proposes that we simply mature over time as you'll see in the Brain Development Chapter.

In other words, we develop because of biological factors.

What Are The Main Questions In Developmental

Psychology?

Overall, developmental psychology aims to answer the questions surrounding human development as discussed.

Although, there are some big questions that are the main focus of developmental psychology. These are:

- What are the primary causes of development? Also known as the nature-nurture debate.
- Is development change qualitative- involves typically changes in structure or organisation or is it:
  - o Quantitative- development is smooth each change building on previous
  - o Discontinuous- development happens in desirable stages.

In other words, One stage must be achieved before the next.

- Or are developmental changes continuous-development is a continuous progression. Build on skills.
- How do skills develop?

This is an interesting question as it proposes that skills could develop in a few different ways. Such as skills could be domain-specific where a specific area of knowledge is organised into a particular domain, as well as development can occur in each area independently of others.

Equally, skills could develop to be domain-general. This is where skills in one area of knowledge are applied in other areas.

So now that we've been introduced into Developmental Psychology, it poses another question: How do we currently think child develop.

Modern Theories of Child Development:

As we go through the book, you'll see great examples of some of the older developmental psychology theories.

However, in recent decades a number of new theories have been developed so that's the focus of this new chapter.

Modern Sociocultural Theory:

If you've read any of my other books or listened to my podcast, then you know I love sociocultural psychology. So, when I came across this theory I was instantly interested.

Therefore, this theory is concerned with the social and historical aspects of human behaviour, and the theory views humans as different from other animals.

Meaning we developed very differently from other animals.

In addition, we are motivated and we have a tendency to teach our offspring, learn from others and humans use language to communicate and use other cultural tools.

Overall, this theory is focused on what motivates us to teach our offspring and how humans use cultural tools to survive as well as develop.

Cultural Intelligence Hypothesis:

Whereas the last theory focused on social and cultural psychology, this focuses on cultural psychology and the big question of What makes us human?

The theory was developed by Herrmann et al (2007) and this theory is made up of a lot of components.

Firstly, humans have Theory of Mind, there's a chapter dedicated to it later, where humans compared to other animals have a set of social cognitive abilities that develop early on in life, and these abilities allow us to have exclusive knowledge with others.

Secondly, humans have shared intentionality. Which is our ability to participate in collaborative activities with shared goals and intentions.

Nonetheless, this depends on the person's ability to read the intent of others, their ability to learn about the culture they live in, for example, the social norms, and they need to be motivated to share psychological states with others.

Penultimately, the theory focuses on the role of instructional learning in the role of development. This is similar to social learning theory where we learn by watching others.

Also, collaborative learning is involved, and this is another term for group learning as well as learning from others.

Finally, the theory explains the role of cultural intelligence and its role in child development. Since our cultural intelligence can develop in two ways.

Firstly, we can learn about culture through understanding agents as goal-directed. We share this method with apes.

This method is similar to social cognitive theory because you get to watch others and learn about the culture through them. Like: what you need to do in a certain context as well as the social norms.

Secondly, humans can learn about the culture by being motivated to share emotional experiences and activities with others. This is unique to humans.

Furthermore, we learn about culture through our interactions with others by the process of imitation, collaborative learning and pedagogy.

The last term means an approach to teaching.

If the above sounds complex because we need to watch people to learn about them and then a lot of other psychological processes occur. I should add our cultural learning isn't fix because it can change over time.

This could happen because of our experience with the social world. For example, if in the culture of your local area it's okay to speak in dialect and informally. But you moved to a posh area and you were shunned by that culture for your dialect. Then the experience with the social world would make you adapt to this new culture.

Another two reasons why this can occur is because of the brain developing and reaching maturation as well as cognitive development occurring.

You'll see this explained more in a few chapters time.

Modern Nativism: Core Knowledge

This theory focuses on human development in terms of our evolutionary history.

For instance, how some primary biological activities evolved. Like: our cognitive skills are determined by evolution and this can be seen in Social cognition.

Please see Cognitive Psychology for more information.

Although, the theory looks at how secondary activities, like cognitive skills, are determined by our culture.

And yes, I was confused as well by the theory classing cognitive skills as primary and secondary. But the theory looks at what is a result of evolution and what's a result of culture.

An example of these secondary activities is the process of acculturation and enculturation.

In short, this is how people adapt to a new culture and how they leave their old cultural identity behind, but I talk more about it in Social Psychology.

Moving onto the next part of the theory, this theory places an emphasis on core knowledge and core systems, with different types of specific systems.

For instance, the theory proposes humans have core domain-specific where each of these systems represent only a small subset of the world. This can be considered as the process of categorisation.

Also, humans have task-specific systems which function to solve a problem.

However, the most important thing to note about this system is the theory labels them as encapsulated. Meaning each system functions relatively independently of one another.

Personally, I'm a bit unsure of this theory because it seems a bit out there but there's some interesting evidence to support this theory.

Evidence:

Firstly, children have surprisingly competent core systems that continue to exist in adulthood, as well as there's evidence of these systems in non-human animals. Suggesting the importance of these systems to our evolution.

Additionally, Wynn (1992) found humans have a core knowledge of numbers in people as young as 5 months old.

Modern Constructivism:

This is our last developmental psychology theory and it's probably the wording of the theory but I'm unsure about it.

Because the theory describes children as a scientist and my problem is that invokes images of children in white lab coats exploring the world.

Anyway, my problems aside, this theory proposes children are scientists that are born with innate theories of the world but these can be revised.

Moreover, when we see children crawling around and investigating their environmental. They're exploring the world and gathering evidence to test their theory's predictions. (Gopnik & Wellmen, 2012)

Again, I know it's probably the wording, but you'll see later in the book this might not be the case.

Building upon this further, the theory proposes children have several different types of theories.

Such as they can have structure theories that look at coherent, abstract concepts and casual relationships.

Another type of theory is cognitive functions. These allow them to predict, interpret and infer their results, and information about the world.

Nevertheless, it's important to note all these theories have a dynamic feature. Meaning they can change in light of new evidence.

As a result, all these theories are defeasible because any theory even central ones may be revised with enough evidence.

Although, I want to note this is very difficult in reality to change central theories as outlined in most of Social Psychology with the role of Implicit Attitudes that are quick to activate and hard to change. (Katz, 1960)

Bayesian Learning:

According to the idea of Bayesian learning, children can learn through revising their theories based upon the assessed probabilities of possibility. As well as Bayes' theories tells us how to revise our beliefs given new evidence.

Overall, the theory proposes our knowledge comes from innate theories, but they can be revised.

Due to new evidence and our theories change over time regardless. As a result of social learning, or when the child observes others and collects new evidence that is used to make new theories.

CHAPTER 2: RESEARCH METHODS IN DEVELOPMENTAL PSYCHOLOGY

As with all subfields of psychology, the different methods that are used to research human behaviour are very important.

Nonetheless, the research methods in developmental psychology are especially innovative and unique as you need to research children, and they aren't always easy to research!

This raises the question of how do you research with children?

One of the many ways that you can research children is by using neuroscience methods. Like: using brain imaging but this only tells us what is happening physically and biologically.

Therefore, it's useless if we want to know about the development of morality.

Another method of researching with children is to use more adult methods but these have quite a few limitations. Like: interviews and questionnaires.

So that was a little introduction to how we can research with children, but why is researching with children so difficult?

Limitations with Children:

One of the problems is that questionnaires don't work for 4 years olds for a few reasons. For example, they're boring, children need to be engaged and they need to understand what the question is asking.

For instance, if you ask a child "What's 1+1?" that sounds very easy to us but a child needs to understand what the + symbol means.

This doesn't tend to happen until the age of 7 when they learn addition at school.

Consequently, when testing with children you need to be more practical and less abstract because you'll see in a later chapter that children deal in practical terms and not abstract terms until later life.

Additionally, you need to be very creative and careful when you say children can't do something, as this can have consequences.

Other difficulties in researching with children include: participants need to be able to show the behaviour you're researching and your desired behaviour may not develop until adolescence or even adulthood.

Another difficulty is that it depends on the child if you get a sensible answer.

Finally, you need to be ethical as it was once thought that babies didn't experience pain, so we can all imagine the type of research done to them.

What Can Infants Do?

Knowing that a limitation of research is that infants might not be able to do your desired behaviour. It poses the question of what can infants do?

This is important to know as this can help you design your experiment accordingly.

Thus, infants can make faces, suck things and look at things in short.

Putting this knowledge into practice, if we make test faces then this can help us to conduct research as infants can sort of control their facial expressions when provided with a stimulus that encourages expression.

Then if the infant adjusts their expression then this would mean they can respond to the stimulus. Leading to inferences. Like: smiling.

Although, it must be noted that interpretation is important and you must make sure that you can interpret the results correctly.

Going back to the smiling interpretation, at 2 months old, an infant will smile at people and if the other person smiles back or reinforces the smile in another way. Then this reinforcement makes it a social smile.

Note: for a social smile to occur in blind babies they need different feedback or a reinforcer.

Sucking on Things as A Measure:

Another measure of a child's behaviour is sucking because children can control the rate that they suck so this rate of sucking can be useful to us.

For example, in experiments, we can use non-nutritive sucking and it's important not to use food, so only information is influencing them.

In addition, we can use this method in experiments due to babies are happy to suck on a pacifier, as well as babies can adjust their sucking rate so when they can see a picture of their mother. They suck faster as they prefer to see pictures of their mother compared to a stranger.

We don't know why, but it's probably due to familiarity.

Looking Behaviour:

An additional way to measure an infant's behaviour is to measure what they're looking at because infants have control over their eye movements.

Thus, we can follow their eyes and measure boredom as well as other things.

One of these methods using looking behaviour is glaze following as we can move stimuli; like a still toy and a moving toy; to see if the infant responds to the movement and we can see if they respond differently between the toys.

In real life, this can be seen if you show an infant two wooden spoons; one with a face on it and one without a face on it; as the infant will follow the faced spoon.

This is even supported with a scrambled face on the spoon.

Equally, we can use looking behaviour to measure boredom using the Habituation/ Dishabituation paradigm.

In short when a baby gets use to looking at something. They become disinterested and bored. This is basically dishabituation.

The research methods works by you show

something to the infant until they get bored then you show them something new, and if they start looking again then they can tell the difference between the old and new object.

Meaning they have formed two separate categories for the two items.

Preferences:

As briefly touched upon in the last few sections, babies can 'recognise' faces they have seen before at the age of 1 month old and from eye-tracking research; where we can see what they're looking at; we can see that children are drawn to faces.

Considerations for Designing A Study in Developmental Psychology:

Let's face it with everything that I have described, explained and spoken about in this chapter. I can probably guess that most of you are panicking, rolling your eyes or have even skipped this chapter because designing an experiment or researching child development is hard!

To be honest, this chapter is one of the reasons why I have absolutely no intention of becoming a developmental psychologist in the future.

I'm more interested in mental health and mental conditions.

Nonetheless, out of my respect and pure admiration for those of you who are still reading this chapter. I will now discuss a few considerations that you should or need to think about when you design your experiment.

Ethical Considerations:

Firstly, you need to think about the ethics of your research and does it follow the British Psychological Society's (BPS) and the American Psychology Association's (APA) ethical guidelines.

If it doesn't then you need to change your study, so it does.

To make your experiment ethical and we're using the BPS' guidelines here; you need to:

- Have respect for the participant and their dignity.
- Your study needs to have scientific value so you can't do a study for the hell of it.
- You need to be socially responsible when designing your study.
- Your study needs to minimise both physiological and psychological harm to the participant.

This is a reason why informed consent is constantly used in psychology as part of these ethical guidelines.

However, getting consent from a child is difficult for a few reasons. Like: they might not be able to appreciate the potential harm the experiment could do to them or they might just agree because they feel like they need to please the experimenters.

This is a massive problem in developmental psychology.

As a result, adults have to consent for them, and this is called assent.

On the other hand, what if you're researching children who have a mental condition, learning disability or another condition that prevents them from understanding or giving informed consent?

Does this mean that you aren't able to research that population?

I'll definitely admit that it's hard to research this population, but adults can give consent for these individuals as The Mental Capacity Act allows someone to give consent for them.

Coercion:

To get 'true' behaviour in psychology studies as well as to minimise our error. We need to make sure that coercion and other effects do not occur in our studies.

For a very introductory look at different things

that can impact research please check out <u>Research in Psychology</u> for more information.

Although, it has long been debated if the course credits that university students; like me; have to earn by taking part in research studies count as coercion.

As we have to take part in these experiments in order to pass our course.

<u>Other Considerations:</u>

As you're dealing with children, you need to consider the sustainability of tasks, the questions and language as well as how sustainable is your testing environment.

You need to think about these aspects of your study as a task might be too simple for us but for a child, it may be complex or really boring, and this WILL impact your results.

In addition, you certainly need to consider your testing environment as labs can be very intimidating to children and the power differential between you and the child is another consideration as children tend to aim to please adults.

Finally, your demeanour and presentation matters in psychology research but especially in developmental psychology research. As if children find your demeanour scary or your presentation strange then they will give different answers and your results could be useless.

Especially, if a child wants to run away from you.

It could happen!

CHAPTER 3: THE PERCIEVED LINK BETWEEN THE MMR VACCINE AND AUTISM

For many years now there has been a rumour, myth whatever you want to call it that the MMR vaccine causes Autism.

I've decided to dedicate a very short chapter to it because I truly believe that it's important to focus on it.

But, I will not tell you if the link is right or wrong because everyone is entitled to their own opinion.

However, I will outline the facts to you, and this will be a summarised version of events.

In the wake of a group of parents believing that the MMR vaccine caused their children to develop Autism. They wanted to sue the company making the MMR vaccine. A researcher called: Wakefield decided to research this link.

Also, Wakefield received £55,000 as a research grant to support the lawsuit.

Therefore, he decided to study 12 children and 11 of these children were the children of the claimants.

This means that there were conflicts of interest from the start and I'll explain more in a moment.

In addition, the study had NO or little ethical approval and the children had to experience colonoscopies, lumbar punctures and more.

One of the children even had some of their blood taken for a blood sample at their birthday party.

Personally, this doesn't sound entirely ethical.

Following this, the results of the study were published in the very prestigious Lancet journal.

However, it was later revealed that Wakefield had a massive conflict of interest with the study as Wakefield was trying to patent another single jab vaccine that was in competition with the MMR vaccine.

In other words, if he harmed the reputation of the MMR vaccine then he could become very rich indeed.

After this conflict was revealed 10 of the 12

authors of the research paper retracted their support.

Real-World Impacts:

The effects of this research are massive as it's causing people not to vaccinate their children against measles, mumps and rubella and this is causing cases to increase.

From 57 confirmed cases of measles in the UK in 1997 to 1,400 in 2008.

Furthermore, vaccines only work if there is herd or collective immunity in a population so if less than a certain percentage of a population isn't vaccinated then the vaccines become less effective and there is a very real possibility of measles, mumps and rubella returning to the modern world.

Whether this is in the form of an outbreak, epidemic or a worldwide pandemic is unknown but it is a possibility.

PART ONE:
BRAIN AND COGNITIVE PSYCHOLOGY

CHAPTER 4: BRAIN DEVELOPMENT

Following on from our introductory chapters, we'll start to investigate brain development.

There are three approaches; biological, cognitive and sociocultural; that we have looked at previously in the series and these enable us to look at brain development from three different angles.

- Biological- enables us to focus on how the structure of the brain helps psychological development.
- Cognitive- enables us to explore how cognitive functions develop and in turn how they help with psychological development.
- Sociocultural- enables us to look at how the environment influences development.

One of the ways of studying brain development is by the use of the structure-function relationship. Which is outlined above.

They can study this relationship by studying the brain over time and comparing the structural changes in the brain compared to the cognitive functions.

If the changes coincide with each other then this could possibly be taken as empirical evidence that brain development and cognitive development are linked.

The Processes Of Brain Development:

The way how the brain develops can be divided into the following four stages:

- Neurogenesis- the creation of new neurons (brain cells) and this part of the process finishes just before birth, as well as these brain cells, are overproduced for the natural process of cell death. This occurs later.
- Migration- the brain cells move to their correct location.
- Differentiation- networks develop to connect all the different brain cells.
- Pruning- this is when brain cells and networks get destroyed and recreated. This allows the brain to become more efficient.

Think pruning as getting rid of millions of old roads and replacing them with one single motorway.

Chugani (1999)

- Using 0-12-month-old children that went through a PET scan; brain scan; they investigate glucose metabolism. (chemical reactions involving sugar in the brain)
- The results showed that 0-1-month-old children had their glucose metabolism focused in the primary sensory and motor cortex (part of the brain associated with movement) and the behaviour of the babies were mostly limited to exploring the environment visually.
- 2-4 months old children had increased metabolism in areas of the brain that focused on more advanced functions and the children's behaviour developed to be more complex. Like: hand-eye coordination.
- 8-12 months children had an increased metabolism in the frontal cortex; area of the brain associated with thinking. This, in turn, coincided with the children developing more cognitively complex behaviour.
- In conclusion, it seems that there's a correlation between structural changes in the brain as well as the developmental of psychological functions in the first year.

Critical Thinking:

A positive of this study was that it used a wide range of ages for the study so we can effectively examine how structural changes in the brain can impact psychological development.

However, this study doesn't look at older children. We cannot say with any certainty or supporting data that these changes in glucose metabolism continue after the first year. Therefore, is it possible that this idea of structure-function relationships is only limited to the first year of birth? Without more research, we can't say for sure.

Limitations of Developmental Brain Science (Neuroscience):

Now there are a few problems with studying the brain and stating with 100% certainty that its related to development.

These problems include:

- The ability/ strategy controversy- this means that the difference or weak performance is shown by a child during an experiment could be down to one of two factors. The first being as a result of underdevelopment. The second being that the child is fully developed but chooses a different strategy to solve the problem. Overall, this is a problem for researchers as its hard to tell which factor is responsible for the weak performance. Possibly leading the researchers to draw the wrong conclusions as they choose that the child is underdeveloped when in fact- they could have chosen a different strategy, for instance.

- Maturation/learning controversy- while maturation is the biological process of development. Learning is caused by the child interacting with the environment. This could cause problems for researchers because these two processes are very closely intertwined. It's hard to say if the structural change in the brain is because of the child's biology or because the child has learnt and this causes a change in their brain as a result of neuroplasticity, the changes in the brain as a result of environmental demands. (please refer to Biological Psychology for more information)

There are more but this is only an introduction to developmental psychology.

CHAPTER 5: COGNITIVE PSYCHOLOGY

An interesting and vital part of development, wouldn't you agree?

But how do children's mental processes develop?

In developmental psychology, there are two main theories that we'll be looking at.

<u>Piaget:</u>

This theory states that a child develops through the movement of clearly different stages, to put it simply.

These stages are:

- Sensorimotor stage- this occurs from birth to the age of two years old. This stage can be described as children's reasoning being second to their ability to move and sense things. In simpler terms, babies hit something and see the results of their actions. This is how they think as they cannot visualise or think about the outcome in their minds.

The easiest way to think of this is when a baby hits a tower and it falls over.

- Preoperational stage- tends to happen from about 2-7 years old. This stage can be described as children have some ability to reason in their minds but not fully.

Some of their limits include:

- Egocentrism- the inability to take other people's perspectives into account.
- Irreversibility- when the child can't reverse the sequence of events. For example, I opened the door, walked through the door and closed the door. The child wouldn't be able to put the sequence into the close, walk then open.
- Centration- only focusing on one aspect of the problem.

Leading us onto a case study.

<u>Piaget and Inhelder (1956):</u>

- The child is shown a 3D model of three mountains with some features on them. Like lakes. But the features are only visible from certain angles.

- After the children have looked at the model for a while a doll is introduced.
- Then after being shown some pictures, the child must choose which photo is taken from the doll's perspective.
- If the child has chosen an image that matches their views. It's taken as a sign of cognitive egocentrism.
- Results showed that children about 4 years old almost always choose the picture from their viewpoint. Whereas by the age of 8 they lose this egocentrism and almost always choose the viewpoint of the doll.
- In conclusion, cognitive egocentrism is a function of age.

Critical Thinking:

Whilst, this study has strong internal validity; it measures what it wanted to measure; so we can effectively see how egocentrism develops as time goes on and by extend cognitive development.

The experiment could be biased because the task could be complex and boring to the children as what 4-year-old child wants to look at some mountains and look at pictures. Therefore, the child could have just picked a random photo to get the experiment over with. This is possibly why later research studies have got different results when they used a more engaging setting for the children.

Back to The Theory:

- Concrete operational stage- occurs from 7- 11 years old. This stage can be described as children can only solve problems that involve real objects and can't solve abstract problems. Such as algebra.
- Formal operational stage- 11- 16 years old. This stage is when abstract development is complete as well as mental operations become abstract and reversible.

Criticism of This Theory:

- They fail to consider individual differences.
- The theory states that biological processes are the driving force behind the theory and fail to consider the sociocultural variables. Like: learning.

Vygotsky's Sociocultural Theory:

Overall, this theory focuses on how sociocultural factors can cause cognitive development, but as it's a long theory with many different components. I'll shorten it for you.

Please refer to Social Psychology to explain some aspects of this theory in further detail.

In its simplest form, the theory states that a child's cognitive development is nothing more than the child learning its own culture and showing the cultural traits of the culture. Better known as internalizing its own culture.

This is done through language where the child learns how the culture speaks in terms of the words themselves and the structure of the language.

In addition, to the interaction with more knowledgeable peers. For example: watching and learning from parents and other models.

Then the theory states that the development of higher-order cognitive functions like thinking and reasoning are mastered using tools. Such as: memorising a list of words written on flashcards.

CHAPTER 6: INTRODUCTION TO THEORY OF MIND

This chapter should be a short one.

Empathy is the ability to understand what others are feeling and experiencing.

Furthermore, empathy is forged from an emotional part; the feeling of what others are; as well as a cognitive part, being able to process what others are experiencing.

While, the theory of mind is about the ability to understand other people's beliefs, perspectives and intentions.

The theory of mind is both wider and narrower than empathy. It's wider as the theory focuses on more than feelings and experiences.

Yet it's narrower as it doesn't consider the emotion like empathy does.

However, both of them are very important as they both help us to understand the experiences of others.

Theory Of Mind And Social Cognition:

A person has theory of mind if they can ascribe mental states to themselves and others. For example, you can tell if someone else is sad or happy, as well as this is a system of inferences that people need to make as we are inferring what that person is feeling.

For instance, you could infer that someone is happy because they are smiling and they're laughing.

Note: this is referred to as theory because such states are not directly observable, and the system can be used to make predictions about the behaviour of others. (Premack & Woodruff, 1978, p515)

What's The Point of The Theory of Mind?

The reason why the Theory of mind is useful in our lives is that it allows us to predict the actions of others and it allows us to understand the goals, desires and intentions of others.

Which is useful for obvious survival reasons!

But most importantly it allows us to understand the beliefs of others and this is the Theory of Mind.

Yet humans can't help seeing goals as by the age

of 6 months we notice that people have goals.

A personal example of this was my nephew saw that my brother was looking for something (his goal) so rather entertainingly my nephew started to pass my brother everything he could see in order to help.

Saying that by 18 months, we appreciate that sometimes human have failed goals, as well as 18-month-old babies, try to help people to complete the failed goal, yet they try to copy the intended behaviour as well.

For example, if a person fails to pick up all the spilt popcorn on the floor but the person can't bend down to pick it up (the failed goal) then the baby could see the intended behaviour of picking up the popcorn and try and help.

Note: this copying is unique to humans.

Desires:

Interestingly, babies have some understanding that different people have different desires to them because if you've ever been around young babies then you probably know that they think that you want a drink after they've finished their drink.

The number of times my nephew wanted me to have some of his drink after he had finished with. It was funny.

Therefore, at 14 months old, babies gave what they preferred but at 18 months, infants gave what others preferred.

Such as a baby might prefer a juice bottle at 14 months so they could pass this to you, but at 18 months they are more likely to pass you your favourite mug or something.

Consequently, this suggests that at some level infants can understand others have different attitudes.

Note on Perspectives:

Another aspect to Theory of Mind is perspectives and this links into egocentrism, that was spoken about in the Cognitive Development chapter, as this involves understanding that others have different views to you.

Thus, as shown in that chapter this aspect of the Theory of Mind could potentially take years to develop during early childhood.

Baron-Cohen, Leslie and Frith (1985)

- Clinically normal children, children with Down Syndrome and autistic children all did the Sally- Anne task.
- The task is a narrative story in simple terms to see if children can understand false beliefs.

- The narrative goes that Sally has a basket and a marble but Anne has a box.
- Sally puts her marble in the basket and goes for a walk.
- When she's away, Anne puts the marble in her box.
- When Sally comes back she looks for her marble.
- Then the question you ask is: where does Sally look for her marble.
- Then if the child doesn't understand false beliefs they will say the box.
- Results showed that 86% of clinically normal children and 85% of children with Down syndrome passed the task. Compared to only 20% autistic children.
- In conclusion, human children normally acquire the ability to represent false beliefs around the age of 4-5 years old.

Critical Thinking:

This study uses a number of groups in their sample so we can see the effects of false beliefs in a number of different groups of children. This increases the creditability of the study has it creates more data for the researchers to support their conclusions with.

Nonetheless, a weakness of this study is that children with ASD did the same experiment as the clinically *normal*; hate that word; children, but it is possible that if the ASD children did a slightly modified version of the experiment so it's more ASD friendly then the rate of them passing could increase? We cannot say for certain without further research.

PART TWO: ATTACHMENT, GENDER IDENTITY, PEERS AND PLAY AND THE SELF

CONNOR WHITELEY

CHAPTER 7: DEVELOPMENT OF THE SELF CONCEPT

When I was taught these next two topics at university, I must admit that I hated them for two reasons. The first being that the lecturer I found quite boring and the second is that I considered this an interesting topic; a loose term; but a waste of my time. As I am fine if a biologically male person identifies as a female person and vice versa.

The reason being that 'male', 'female' and all genders are mere constructs that society has created.

For example, what is a chef?

Why is a chef called a chef instead of a Police Officer?

The only reason is that society has created two different labels for these two different jobs.

And gender is the same thing.

In addition, I think that if people are arguing and moaning about people just because of their non-traditional gender. Then they're wasting their time when they could thinking and arguing about more important topics and threats to society.

The Topic:

Anyway, onto the topic then- all social identities are based on the idea that people are what they identify themselves as. For instance: I am a teacher, I am a boy and I am a mother.

I would recommend reading Social Psychology and reading the chapters on Social Cognitive Theory and Social Identity Theory as well as The Self for more information on this topic.

Furthermore, social roles are a set of expectations about a person's behaviour as a result of belonging to a group.

An example of this is that a boy may believe that his social role is to be the breadwinner of his family because he belongs to a society where men should be on the most income to support his family.

Or a woman believes that her social role is to stay at home and have children because she belongs to a group or society that believes that women should stay at home and not get jobs.

In addition, our sense of social identity comes from a number of feeling, thinking as well as behavioural components. (Tajfel, 1978) as well as the self-concept are ideas we have about ourselves including our physical and mental qualities as well as our behavioural and emotional attributes.

Interestingly, there has been a lot of research into how children perceive themselves.

Therefore, when it comes to self-concept throughout childhood and when children were asked the 'who am I?' question. Children who are 5 or under focus on their physical features or facts to form their self-concept. Like: I am a boy and I've got a toy car.

In addition, during this early infancy period, children don't have an awareness of the self. After all, they don't perceive themselves as distinct human beings because they don't understand their uniqueness (appearance and properties) and that they have an effect on the world.

Although, between the ages of five and nine years old, children make more character references, as well as interpersonal traits, are sometimes used by children when describing the self.

For example, 'I am a happy person, but sometimes I am shy'

Finally, beyond the age of 10 years old, children add a lot of qualities by considering their private self-knowledge.

For example: 'I try not to be greedy but it is hard at times'

Although, there are other types of the Self that children must discover as each of these Selves impact the child in different ways. For example:

- Subjective or existential self- the recognition of the self as a unique and distinctive being that differs from others as well as this has an element of self-referencing.
- Objective or categorical self-the recognition of the self as the person seen by others and defined by the attributes and qualities used to define groups.

In other words, the child recognises how other people perceive them.

- Looking glass self- the sense of self we develop to respond to interaction with others and see how others react to us.

A child's self-concept is highly influenced by their social development.

This social development starts off as a rudimentary feeling before it develops into a more complex understanding of how the social world works.

The self-concept develops from an extremely rough understanding of their existence as an independent entity to a more evaluative as well as reflective self-concept due to the child being aware of how they're perceived by others.

Although, this is influenced by the child's interaction with peers and others.

Self-Concept at Different Ages:

As with everything in Developmental Psychology and behaviour in general, different behaviours manifest or develop at different stages- and Self-concept is no exception.

As a result, between the ages of 3-5 years old, children tend to focus on concrete physical descriptions when describing themselves. (Harter, 1996) As children are only aware of themselves in the physical sense.

Whereas, between the ages of 5-9 years old, children can describe themselves using qualifiers as children are engaging in social comparison (Bulter, 1998)

Such as: "I am good for sports and I am bad for maths,"

Finally, during Adolescence, children can start to

define themselves using abstract concepts and they use more qualifiers. Like: "I am extremely smart and I am really quick,"

Aspects of the self:

William (1980) proposed that two distinct aspects of the self exist. These aspects are the I self and Self-esteem.

Although, in this book, we'll focus on the development of the I Self as this is the more interesting and the less complex aspect of the Self to discuss.

However, if you want to learn more about Self-Esteem, please check out Social Psychology for more information.

Early Development of I Self:

Many theorists argue that we can see the I self develop when we can see the effect we have on the world.

For example, we can understand that we are a separate unique entity to the world when we can push over a tower of blocks so they fall and understand that WE caused the blocks to fall.

So now that we understand how we develop a sense of who we are, it begs the question: How do we develop a sense of what gender we are?

CHAPTER 8: GENDER IDENTITY

Continuing on from our last chapter, we'll be looking at the concept of gender and gender is a very interesting idea as gender is one of the first social groups that children understand, as well as these stereotypes, are very strong in earlier childhood but their strength decreases in middle schooling years.

In addition, it is interesting to think about how strongly gender stereotypes have persisted despite the dramatic changes there have been to society through the centuries, as well as gender stereotypes incorporate the personalities role as well as abilities of women and men.

But this raises the questions of how do children begin to understand the social group of gender and what are Gender Identities?

What is Gender Identity?

Gender identity refers to the self-perception of male, female or other genders and gender identity is a part of the social identity and they come from the internalizing of gender roles.

Gender Identity Development:

To help explain how a child's gender identity; so how a boy or girl develops their perceived identity as a boy or girl; develops is the theory known as Kohlberg's theory (1966) which proposes that children move through 3 stages and by 6 or 7 years old they obtain gender constancy.

In other words, the child knows that gender is 'fixed' and they can only be one gender.

Therefore, the three stages are:

Stage 1: Gender Labelling

This stage occurs between the ages of 2-3 and a half years old and at this stage children can label their own sex and others, but children cannot understand that gender is constant over time or changes in a gender's appearance.

Stage 2: Gender Stability

Between the ages of 3.5-4.5 years old, children develop some understanding that gender is constant over time but still needs to fully understand it and the changes in appearance that the two genders go through.

Stage 3 Gender Constancy:

Finally, between the ages of 4.5- 7 years old despite changes between the genders; like the differences between a girl and woman; children understand that gender is biologically based and it remains the same throughout the human lifespan.

Causes of Gender Identity:

After looking at that interesting theory about the development of gender identity, we're now going to look at the different factors and reasons for why gender develops from a biological, cognitive and social standpoint. As each perspective gives us another explanation for how our concept of gender is formed.

Biological Reasons:

During the prenatal stage of pregnancy, the body secretes sex-determining hormones and being exposed to these hormones has long term effects on the mind and body.

- Hines (2004)- found that girls with a genetic disorder giving them higher levels of testosterone in their blood. Typically engaged in more male-like behaviour than typically found in girls.
- Goy and McEwen (1980)- found the same as the study above but by injecting pregnant rats with testosterone.

Genes can play a role in producing atypical behaviour in people because genetic conditions can produce behaviour that isn't usual for that gender.

Usually, females have two X chromosomes; it's a part of your genes, and males have one X and one Y chromosome.

- Turner's syndrome- when females are missing the second X chromosome.
- Klinefelter's syndrome- when males have an extra X chromosome.

<u>Cognitive Reasons:</u>

There are two main theories about gender from a cognitive standpoint.

- Kohlberg's cognitive developmental theory- this theory states that the development of gender identity is triggered by gender constancy; the idea that gender is fixed and unchangeable; and over time it becomes more and more fixed to form an identity.

Slaby and Frey (1975)

- To investigate the role of gender constancy, the researchers assessed 55 2-5-year-old children with an interview to see the gender constancy of the child.
- Then the children were shown a video with a man and a woman doing the same tasks. Like: building a fire and drinking juice.
- The dependent variable of the experiment was to see how long the child-focused on same-sex models.
- Results showed that children with higher levels of gender constancy have more selective attention for same-sex models.
- For example, boys with lower gender constancy focused on male models about 48% of the time whereas boys with higher levels focused on same-sex models for about 61% of the time.
- The same was true for girls.
- In conclusion, gender constancy is an important milestone in a child's development in terms of gender identity as it triggers selective attention to same-sex models.

Critical Thinking:

The study used a reasonably large sample size so they could generate more data to support and draw their conclusions from. This increases the reliability of the study.

Nevertheless, this study does lack ecological validity; how the results of the experiment can be applied to the real world; because children don't typically watch models on a film doing tasks. In the real world, children see and learn from models by watching them in a natural setting. Furthermore, in this natural setting, there are other engaging or interesting things going on in this environment that wasn't happening in the film. For example, the model may talk to the child, there will be a non-visual sensory stimulus in the environment and other factors that could impact gender constancy.

Gender Schema Theory:

I recommend reading Cognitive Psychology 2nd Edition to further understand schema theory.

According to this theory, the development of gender identity is triggered by gender labelling and schematic processing.

In other words, it's triggered by labelling tasks to specific genders as well as processing information in a way that it's affected by a mental representation or framework about what a particular gender is meant to be.

This partly explains why lesbians are thought of as abnormal by some people. As the concept of women loving women and sometimes being strong and masculine goes against the schema of what women typically are.

Social Reasons:

The main social factors that cause gender identity to develop is gender socialisation by peers and parents.

This is children internalising social norms about a gender's behaviour.

This factor is strongly linked to Social Cognitive Theory as the children watch their models and learn from their model's behaviour.

Overall, this leads to gender identity being formed because as the children watch their models, they begin to learn about gender roles and gender behaviour. Then they use what their models have directly or indirectly taught them and start to behave similarly.

Influence of Parents:

Parents have a big impact on the development of their child's gender identity as parents view their children in stereotypical ways and as humans, we all tend to stereotype children more than adults. Leading to parents creating a gender-stereotypical environment. Like: a pink princess bedroom for girls. This helps to reinforce and influence the child's gender identity.

Finally, and perhaps the biggest way how parents influence their child's gender identity is through their strong discouragement of counter stereotypical behaviour. For example, a parent may shout or moan at their son for wanting to play with dolls or a girl for wanting to be an engineer.

CHAPTER 9: INTRODUCTION TO ATTACHMENT

This has to be one of the most important behaviours in 'good' child development as being attached to someone is important for many reasons.

Attachment refers to the emotional bond between the child as well as the caregiver (or another person if you wanted to create a universal definition and not a developmental one) that presents itself as being calm in their presence and distressed when not in their presence, as well as here's another great definition for Attachment:

"There is no such thing as a baby ... if you set out to describe a baby, you will find you are describing a baby and someone. A baby cannot exist alone, but is essentially part of a relationship"

(Winnicott, 1964, p. 88),

As you can see from the quote above and from

1

everyday life, babies don't exist alone and babies need to find a balance between exploring their own environment; which could be dangerous; and safety.

This highlights the importance of attachment as attachments help us to find this balance, as well as attachment, has critical survival and adaptation values.

In practical terms, it means that caregivers can stop you before you spill boiling hot tea on yourself.

Furthermore, attachments aim to provide nurturement as well as provide protection for your physiological and psychological security.

Theories of Attachment:

Before we explore the great work of Bowlby and Harlow on attachment, I wanted to quickly mention two theories of attachment that predate our modern thinking.

So, Freud believed in a Drive-reduction explanation of attachment. Meaning that we form attachments because our attachment figure provides us with our drive. Leading our drive or want to be reduced so we bond with them.

Let's use an example.

According to the theory, when a baby is hungry (this is a drive) and a mother gives them food (meaning they reduce their drive) the baby would experience pleasure.

Leading the baby to associate the mother with pleasure and the baby would become attached to the mother.

Imprint: (Lorenz)

According to this idea, new-borns of most species recognise and seek proximity to the first object that they encounter as long as it's moving.

Leading to the animal becoming attached to the first thing that they saw, but there is a critical period to imprinting and once an imprint has occurred it cannot be undone.

The Biological Basis for Attachment:

After looking at the two ideas, we're now going to be looking at the great work of Harlow and Bowlby.

Therefore, Harlow (1958) was a researcher who set out to find a biological explanation for attachment.

He conducted two experiments.

The first experiment found that attachment is driven by contact comfort and not the satisfaction of basic needs.

For example, a child forms attachment because they are comfortable around you and not because you provide their basic needs.

Off the top of my head, this explains and is further supported by the reason why a kidnap victim doesn't always form an attachment to their kidnapper that effectively looks after them.

The second experiment is detailed below:

Harlow (1958)

- Baby monkeys were placed in a room filled with toys to play with. Interacting with a rich environment is important to cognitive development.
- In three conditions the monkeys were left in the room alone, with a mother made from wire or a mother made from cloth.
- Results showed that the monkeys explored the environment more with the cloth mother as they used it as a secure base. While in the other two conditions they were much more likely to freeze or go into the corner and cry.

Critical Thinking:

The experiment has an effective method for measuring this hypothesis, so this increases the reliability of the results.

Although, the reliability of the results could be

called into question as it used animals and it's still hotly debated whether or not the animal and human behaviours are the same. Thus, the results of the experiment could only apply to monkeys as they were used in the experiment or the results could in fact only apply to humans to a certain extent, unless a follow-up experiment is done using human children we cannot say for sure if this hypothesis applies to humans.

Attachment in Humans:

John Bowlby was the first researcher to formulate a theory about why attachment occurs.

His theory includes two components:

- Attachment behavioural system- referring to the pre-programmed instincts we have that are biologically encoded in us. These instincts are behaviours that occur in response to certain environmental triggers.
- Internal Working Model- referring to the psychological aspects of attachment. These include beliefs about the self, the caregiver as well as the relationship with the caregiver.

Bowlby believed that the internal working model is formed in early childhood and it influences future relationships.

For example: if your caregivers constantly neglect

you despite you trying your best to get their attention. This could lead to the development of feelings of worthlessness. Possibly affecting your future relationships as you could always be trying to prove yourself worthy of your friends or partner's attention, or you could become an attention seeker.

Building upon this further, the Internal Working Model includes the set of expectations that you have about the attachment figure.

For example, your expectations when you think about

- Will they be there when I need support?
- How will they make me feel?

Parting Note:

Wait, I've only explained the theories of attachment, but how do you acquire attachment and what are the types of attachment that people can have?

CHAPTER 10: ACQUIRING ATTACHMENT AND TYPES OF ATTACHMENT

Following our look at what attachment is and how it's formed, this leads us to the question of how does someone acquire attachment?

To answer this question, research has shown that attachment is acquired through a number of stages that occur at different ages.

These different stages include:

- Preattachment (6 weeks)- recognises mum but not yet all mates. Produce innate signals to summon caregiver. Like: crying.
- Early attachment (to 7 months) orients to a particular individual, preference for the family caregiver.
- Separation protest (9 months to 2 years) the child seeks contact with the caregiver and becomes anxious when separated.

- Goal corrected: (2+ years)- This is whether the child negotiates with caregivers to accommodate his or her needs as well as both the child and caregiver share responsibility for maintaining contact.

Moreover, this skill develops around the same time as mental representation skills, and as mentioned in the last chapter at this stage children have a developed an internal working model to guide the relationship. This helps them to know where they fit in the world.

For more information on mental representations and their importance in thinking. Please check out Cognitive Psychology 2nd Edition.

Types of Attachment:

When you really think about people and the relationships that they have with different people. It will probably come as no surprise that there are different types of attachment and each of these types is characterized by different feelings towards the caregiver.

For example, the Avoidant attachment type has a prevalence or commonality of 20% in the western population and it is characterised as a person not being distressed by separation and reunion, as well as they consciously avoid interaction with the caregiver.

Another attachment type is called: Secure Attachment; which makes up about 70% of the Western Population and this is where the child explores their environment and uses the mother as a secure base, they maintain proximity and interaction as well as they experience separation anxiety.

The final attachment type is Resistant; this makes up 10% of the Western population; and this is where the child is clingy, experiences distress when separated, but they are difficult to comfort, as well as on reunion with their caregiver they are both seeking and resisting contact.

In addition, these attachment types can be seen in adults as you model your caregivers and use the knowledge and experiences of attachment and peer relations to guide your future relationships.

Lastly, there is a miscellaneous attachment type where there is a lack of a coherent strategy to handle stress.

By strategy to handle stress, I mean that Secure attachment people go to the Caregiver whenever they need comfort and resistant people don't go to the caregiver for comfort.

But these miscellaneous attachment people, don't have one strategy that they constantly use to comfort themselves.

Types of Attachment in Interviews:

Interestingly, when you're interviewed or questioned about your life your answers can be influenced by your attachment style.

For example, in interviews, people with a secure attachment style acknowledged the importance of close relationships, talk freely about past and present attachments as well as they have an insight into the emotion of others.

Whereas, people with the Insecure Avoidant Attachment Style believed what happened in their childhood is not important and personal relationships are not very important as well as they provide sparse, little detail and an unemotional response.

Finally, people with an insecure resistant attachment style produced lengthy interviews with no clear structure. Where they acknowledged past experiences, but they haven't resolved them. Also, they spoke about past events almost as if they were reliving them.

Interestingly, these attachment styles are relatively stable as Waters et al (2000) showed that 72% of adults kept their attachment classification over a 20-year span.

This is because a person's internal working model is hard to change as they are based on expectations and patterns that develop during childhood.

Cultural Variation:

As you'll see in a later chapter, culture has massive impacts on our development and attachment is no exception as Japanese and Korean infants have different types of insecure attachment. (Takahashi, 1990; Jin et al, 2012) as well as cultural differences around mother-infant closeness; where it may be greater or weaker in a particular culture; and cultural differences in daycare. All play a role in the development of a particular attachment type.

But I wonder how relationships and feelings affect attachment?

CHAPTER 11: RELATIONSHIPS, FEELINGS AND ATTACHMENT TYPES

After learning about the different attachment types you can have, it's important to recognise that each of these types of attachment can impact relationships differently and how the child can feel about the caregiver.

Two quick examples would be a person with Secure attachment would say: "I can call for comfort and I am worthy of receiving it,"

However, a person with a resistant attachment would say "I am sometimes worthy of attention but not always. Sometimes when I'm distress, I have to comfort my caregiver."

Hence, showing the differences in beliefs that different attachment styles can cause.

Although, attachment types can have other impacts and beliefs as well. For instance:

- Secure- my caregiver is often available and will return to me. I am loveable and worthy.
- Insecure (Avoidant) - my caregiver is rejecting. I have to be self-reliant and emotionally strong. I don't feel safe with others and don't like to be dependent on them.
- Insecure (resistant)- my caregiver is cold and I'm unloved.

Although, what factors in a caregiver's life can impact these attachment outcomes for their child?

Some include:

- Mental Health Conditions
- Secure consistently responsive
- Parental sensitivity
- Mind-minded- seeing their child as an individual with thoughts and feeling and not an object, as well as being able to understand a story or life from their child's perspective.

Factors That Cause Resistant and Inconsistent Attachment:

I'll definitely admit that attachment is mainly environmentally determined, but I wonder what causes each type of attachment?

Note: when I started to write these later sections I thought that it would be helpful to remind people that the factors given below that cause the less favourable types of attachment do not make these caregivers bad people. As sometimes these factors can be caused by no fault of the caregiver.

For example, depression and other mental health conditions.

In other words, it's important to consider a person's situation and circumstance.

Sadly for this type of attachment, caregivers tend to only respond sometimes to their child's actions and they can sometimes be overbearing.

In response to this by the age of 3-6 years old the child often tries to control the caregiver's activities to try and get this attention.

This can be by being overly helpful or aggressive (Moss et al, 2004)

A Quick Note on Day-care and Attachment:

According to Belsky et al (2007), if a child spends more than 20 hours a week at day-care then they are more likely to have an insecure attachment to their caregivers.

On the other hand, if there's a bad situation at home, day-care can improve attachment.

Long Term Effects of Attachment:

The long term effects of having a secure attachment style tend to include adjusting better to situations, having better social skills and having closer relationships with peers.

Furthermore, these people tend to be less depressed, anxious and less socially withdrawn, less delinquent and aggressive as well as they have higher self-esteem.

Whereas people with the insecure-avoidant attachment style tend to have less social support, they are more likely to have earlier sexual experiences and engage in more risky sexual behaviour.

A possible reason for this could be people with a secure attachment style might develop more positive internal working models so they may be happy to express emotion and seek support.

Whereas insecure children might have learned to inhibit emotional expressively and they may seek comfort, due to their internal working model being different.

CHAPTER 12: INTRODUCTION TO PEERS AND PLAY

Play and interaction with peers are undeniable for helping children develop, but how exactly does it help development?

Play develops as the child grows and gets older.

For example: at ages 1-2 years old the type of play is object manipulation when the child is only interested in the object itself as well as its properties. Like colours, shape and texture.

At ages 3-5 years old, the type of play changes to pretend play when the child uses objects as symbols to act out a pretend social role. Like a family dinner. Enabling children to understand the meaning of objects.

At 6-7 years old, the type of play changes for the last time to become play with rules as the child doesn't focus on the object nor the social role it could be used for, instead they focus on rules. This is because rules regulate the social world and complex sequences of social interactions, so they require complex cognitive structures that form at about this age.

Influence of Peers And Play On Cognitive Development:

Linking back to our cognitive development theories, Paiget believed that development in peer interaction is driven by the process of perspective talking, so being in a group of equal peers that find each other relatable would be helpful for development.

Damon and Killen (1982) support this idea as they found that when children talk in groups this promotes moral reasoning more effectively than talking with adults.

Whereas, Vygotsky believed that cognitive development is driven by being around knowledgeable others. This can be parents or peers.

Nedospavosa (1985) supports Vygotsky as they found that 5-7-year-old children overcome egocentrism easier when an adult is present, and they provide just enough help for the child to understand and complete the task. Supporting the idea of knowledgable others is important for cognitive development.

The Influence Of Peers And Play On Social Development:

Interactions with peers and play in childhood create the vital foundation social skills so the child can develop and adjust to social situations in later life.

Hollos and Cowan (1973)

- Children from isolated farms and children from towns in Norway did a number of tasks to measure logical skills; like a conservation task with water; and social skills.
- To see social development in children from isolated farms as these children tend to have no same-aged peers on the farm.
- Results showed while there was no difference in the development of logical skills then there was a clear difference in the development of social skills from children from the isolated farms. Compared to children from the town.
- In conclusion, growing up in an isolated environment with no same-age peers has a negative impact on the development of vital social skills.

Critical Thinking:

A positive of this study is that it has high ecological validity as the experiment uses a natural, real-world setting. In turn, this increases the generalizability of the findings, so we can apply the results of the experiment to different situations.

Whilst, the above is true, a negative of the study is that it only used one area and one culture. Therefore, we cannot say that this is part of a universal behavioural trend with supporting data as the study didn't include other cultures or other geographical areas. As a result of this, this may be a one-off occurrence or something unique to this area.

CHAPTER 13: PEERS AND PLAY

Since infancy, children seem to have an innate curiosity and a need to engage with others, and after looking this topic in an introductory sense, I think that it would be useful to explore the topic of peers and play in more depth.

Especially, as plays and peer relations are vital in child development as well as despite play looking easy, it's actually very difficult because it involves a lot of social and cognitive skills. Also, the skills required to enact a more meaningful and more complex interaction will take some time to develop.

These needed skills include:

- Sharing
- Taking turns
- Understanding perspectives negotiation

Overall, play as a natural and vital aspect of a child's day to day life as well as it's very useful for play and development.

In addition, interactions between adults provide the child with structure and guidance about how to develop these skills.

Moreover, some psychologists believe a child's peer group is the most important factor in development, even more, important than parents.

Development of Peer Groups and Peer Interaction:

In addition, to the types of play and how they develop as examined in the last chapter, we have discovered a lot through studying pairs of infants in labs.

For example, 3-4 months old babies focus on looking and touching others, at 6 months babies babble at others and they direct smiles at peers, between the ages of 1-2 years old babies can coordinate their movements to be able to interact with others as well as they can start to use language when they interact with others from the age of 2-3 years old.

Nonetheless, it must be noted that children prefer to play with objects and they only tend to engage with people when there are no toys around.

In fact, it's only around the age of two that babies seem interested in more elaborate social interactions.

Even then, these interactions can ultimately lead to conflict. (Hay and Ross, 1982) possibly as at this developmental stage, neither party has the needed social skills to tolerant each other's needs for long.

A Summary of Peer Groups and Interaction Throughout Infancy:

As I know that that was a lot of information, I thought that it would be useful to include a shorten summarised version of the information above.

As earlier as 6 months babies show engaging behaviour when they are faced with another baby.

Nevertheless, this behaviour like touching and noise is more obvious by the end of the year. (Hany et al, 1983)

Whilst, it's impossible to state a causal link between play and development.

Play has been linked to the enhancement of certain cognitive and language skills.

For example, the theory of mind as this promotes an emotional standing and leads to more interaction with others.

Interestingly, even physical (non-symbolic) types of play like rough and tumble can establish a hierarchy within a safe space. Possibly leading to more social interaction.

Preschool:

Once a child enters preschool; like nursery; the amount and quality of peer interaction dramatically increase and children get better at communicating understanding thoughts, and feeling of others.

Peer Groups in Adolescence:

In adolescence, peer groups, as well as their related activities, become more important as peer groups have a number of consequences for the self.

As a result, they act as reference point support. Providing guidance on defining the self, as well as they support feelings of self-worth.

Social Development:

Parten (1932) observed 2-4-year-olds and found three distinctive stages in a child's social development.

These three stages were non-social play, true social interaction and development of friendship.

Non-Social Play:

This play is when the child behaves as an onlooker at the other children and plays by themselves.

Furthermore, parallel play can occur at this stage. This is a limited type of play where the child plays using the same material as others but doesn't try to influence play.

For example, two children might both be playing a game involving building sandcastles, but these individuals will be independent of each other instead of playing together.

True Social Interaction:

At this stage, children start to interact with one another and play together. However, they can engage in social interaction in a few different ways.

- Associative play- children engage in separate activities but they interact by commenting on another's behaviour and exchanging toys.
- Cooperative play- children's interaction are directed towards a common goal.

Development of Friendships:

A friendship is a close relationship that involves companionship and the other person wanting to be with you.

For adults, friendships involve trust, companionship and sharing and more.

However, for younger children, these friendships start off as something more concrete. That are usually centred around a particular activity.

Like: a school friendship is centred around the physical entity of a school.

Therefore, friendships can be viewed as developing in 3 stages:

- Stage 1- friendship as a playmate
- Stage 2- friendship is about mutual trust and assistance. The idea of friendship becomes more complex and psychological as well as trust becomes a defining feature.
- Stage 3- friendship is about intimacy and loyalty.

Stage 3 can typically occur in the teenage years and onwards because as previously mentioned in other chapters teenagers can understand abstract concepts like intimacy and loyalty.

Building upon this further, teenagers stress the following in friendships and I personally agree with these qualities as I don't think friendship means that much without them:

- Intimacy- psychological closeness, mutual understand and trust.
- Loyalty- want their friend to defend them and not them for someone else.

Nonetheless, we've looked at what happens when we have friends and how friendships develop, but what happens if you sadly don't have any friends in childhood?

<u>Consequences of Not Having Friends in Childhood:</u>

You can probably guess that there are a few negative consequences of not having friends in childhood.

For example, not having friends can have negative consequences for education later on in life and you might deal worse with stress as during stressful periods you will not have any friends for support.

Nonetheless, just because you have friends during childhood doesn't mean that you're going to be fine in later life.

The reason for this is because our childhood friendships and other relationships provide us with the foundations for future relationships.

In other words, if your friends and other relationships treat you badly then this will certainly impact your later relationships. For instance, you might become more cautious about making friends to avoid getting worse or mistreated again.

Another example of how friendships can potentially harm a person is because some friendships are likely to increase aggression and anti-social behaviour.

Typically, this is referred to as getting in with the wrong crowd.

Rejection in Childhood:

Moving onto rejection in childhood, if a child gets rejected, avoided and disliked by others. This could be because they have poor perspective-taking skills, antagonistic or they could have poor emotional conduct.

However, this lack of peer interaction actually makes these problems worse and these problems are linked to poor developmental outcomes.

For example, in adolescence, they are likely to do less well in schools, drop out of education, be bullied and act out.

CHAPTER 14: PRETEND OR SYMBOLIC PLAY

Continuing with our look at the role of play in developmental psychology in the next few chapters. I want to open this chapter with the United Nations' mandate from 1987.

"Play is the basic right for every child."

I love this quote because it symbolises children deserve to be free, learn and have fun and that's vital in development.

Other Classifications of Play:

In previous chapters, we've looked at types of play but here are a few more.

For example, Sensory-motor play. This is essentially the earliest kind of play when an infant is beginning to produce pleasurable effects. This is what Piaget called 'secondary circular reactions' (like repeatedly banging a toy on the floor)

Furthermore, you have socio-dramatic play. This is a pretend play involving social role play in an extended story sequence of some kind. Like playing doctors or other made up games.

Subsequently, you have symbolic play which occurs around the age of 2, when children play symbolically with various objects, children invoke an imaginative, role-taking component (Tamis-LeMonda et al., 2002). They start enacting roles.

Their play activity here relies on using familiar objects and scenarios. Such as a banana for a telephone, or fantasy-based roles and contexts. Like, acting as a fairy princess in another land.

Piaget's Development of Pretend Play

As always Piaget provides us with an interesting theory to explain things, so in his theory, there are two stages of pretend play with a few substages.

Therefore, stage 1 doesn't take place until the infant is 4 years old as well as in the first substage children play using various props and pretend and imitate actions with them. For instance, when little girls pretend to have tea parties with teddies or imaginary friends.

In the second substage children pretend and imitate without the use of props sometimes. Here children start to use their imagination to play. Such as when princesses, dragons and witches start to appear in their games.

In the third substage, infants start to use more complex symbols in their play.

In Stage 2, which is between 4-7 years old their play becomes more orderly. Children want to imitate reality and they tend to ascribe social roles to the participants of the play. Like the role of teacher, mother or father.

We know from research that symbolic play has effects on cognitive development. With Symbolic play being related to enhanced abstract thought, symbolic representation, perspective taking, creativity, memory, intelligence, language, and literacy, as well as self-regulation. That's when children learn to manage their own behaviours and emotions.

Pretend Play and Language:

There is a lot of research on the correlation between pretend play and language ability.

The idea behind this relationship is according to Piaget (1945/1962) pretending is an early expression of a child's ability to use and understand symbols.

Therefore, an infant's language could develop in parallel with their ability to pretend. Since they both require the use of and comprehension of symbols (Bates et al., 1979; Piaget, 1945/1962)

In addition, research has shown that in children younger than 18 months, pretend play and language production are significantly correlated (Tamis-

LeMonda et al., 1992) As well as children with language delays are less successful at engaging in symbolic play than children at the same age with normally developing language. (Beeghly, 1998)

Another piece of evidence is Lewis et al. (2000) who examined the relationships between pretend play and expressive and receptive language using 40 normally developing 1 to 6-year-olds infants.

To test this, the researchers used the Test of Pretend Play (ToPP) and the Preschool Language Scale-3. (PLS-3)

They found there was a positive correlation between symbolic play and both expressive and receptive language. This could be because symbolic pretend play requires both conceptual knowledge and symbolic skills, as does language.

Overall, the researchers suggested that an infant's ability to pretend may act as a foundation for symbolic play and language development.

Pretend Play and Language Difficulties:

In the last section, we read that pretend play can help language development and vice versa. So, what happens if an infant has language difficulties?

According to Mundy et al. (1987), there's a significant correlation between spontaneous symbolic play and expressive and receptive language in 16 3–6 year-olds with autism. Meaning autistic children can take part in pretend play and use expressive as well as receptive language.

Additionally, Beeghly et al. (1990) compared symbolic play of young children with Down's syndrome with similar mental age typical children. They found a positive relationship between mean length of utterance and symbolic play in both groups. As well as this relationship was stronger in children with Down's syndrome under 5 years. Whereas there was a stronger relationship in the typically developing children over 5 years.

Consequently, if you're as confused as I am when I first read that, it means children with Down's syndrome have the same level of language and pretend play as typically developed children at the same mental, not physical, age.

Finally, Jarrold et al. (1994) argue that Harris and Lillard are correct only for solitary pretend play when a child is alone. Whereas, Leslie is correct for shared pretend play. Since shared pretend play is a lot more complex because you would have to both understand how pretend play works and what the pretend objects is. This is another way for saying you need a meta-understanding of pretend play. For example, you pretend the banana is a telephone and I'll say 'Hello' to you.

On the whole, this argument is in agreement with Lewis et al. who argued that an infant's ability to pretend might be a requirement for solitary symbolic play and the beginning of language.

However, *meta-representation* could be a requirement for shared symbolic play and intentional communication, and not our ability to pretend. (Lewis et al., 2000)

Do Children Understand That Symbols Represent Something From Reality?

I have to admit this sounds strange at first because it's natural to imagine that children don't understand their symbols are based on reality. But psychology is rarely what we think so let's look at the research.

To answer this question, Harris and Kavanaugh (1993) showed 1-2-year-old infants a yellow block and a teddy and told the infants the yellow block was the teddy's sandwich.

Next, they were asked to show what teddy does with his sandwich.

The researchers found the 18-month-olds had their teddy eating the block correctly on 50% of the time. Whereas the 28-month-olds did so on 75% of the time.

As a result, based on these findings the researchers suggested that at this age imitation is limited. As well as it might be the children's pretence comprehension that is mediated by language.

CHAPTER 15: PRETEND PLAY, CREATIVITY, SCAFFOLDING, ROLE TAKING AND IMAGINARY FRIENDS

Pretend Play and Creativity

Continuing to look at pretend play and its many benefits, there's been research into the relationship of pretend play and creativity.

For example, Mottweiler & Taylor (2014) looked at the relationship of role-play and creativity by studying 5 4-5-year-old children. The researchers studied them by interviewing the children and they gave a questionnaire to parents.

Subsequently, they tested the infant's Pretend play ability by asking questions about their imaginary friends, asking them to pretend to be someone else and about performing actions with imaginary objects. Like, pretending to brush their teeth with a toothbrush.

Next, the researchers tested the children's creativity by asking them to provide endings to stories and drawings.

Overall, the study found that children who engaged in more elaborate role play, like playing with imaginary friends and using pretend identities, had higher creativity scores in their narratives.

Therefore, this suggests there's a relationship between pretend play and creativity. But as of yet, there is no research support that pretend play or pretence predicts creativity.

Another study of note is Hoffmann & Russ (2016) when they conducted an intervention study with 50 5-8-year-old females.

In this study, the researchers had children in play sessions twice a week for 3 weeks in groups of 4, as well as the children told stories using the toys provided. But in the control group, children played with beads, puzzles, and colouring books.

They measured creativity within 2 weeks of the end of the intervention, with a story book test and the Alternative Uses Task. Also, play was assessed with the Affect in Play Scale.

After the study, they found that organisation and imagination in pretend play improved a lot in the intervention group compared to the control group. Yet there wasn't significant improvements in creativity in the intervention group compared to the control group. So, more work needed to be done.

Meaning this study found that pretend play has the benefits of making infants more organised and it increases their imagination.

However, it doesn't necessarily increase their creativity.

Role Taking:

After looking at pretend play, we need to look at a sub-feature or another type of play. That's called role-playing or role-taking.

Personally, I loved role-playing as a child whether it be Indiana Jones, doctors or anything else I liked it!

Moving on, role-taking is a specific form of pretend play and it involves the child becoming mentally and emotionally like the characters they're playing.

This is a very important type of play because it helps to promote social Cognition. This, in short, is people thinking about people.

Moreover, there are two types of role-taking. The first is dramatic play. This is pretend play which involves enacting a character by yourself. As sad as it sounds, this is what I did most of the time during my childhood.

Whereas, the second type is called sociodramatic

play where child play together and re-enacting two or more characters.

Role Taking and Theory of Mind:

Interestingly, there's an argument in developmental psychology that there is a relationship between pretend play and theory of mind. Since our ability to understand other people's emotional states involves us, for lack of a better term, having to pretend or role-play with their emotional states. In an effort to understand them.

Also, children have been found to use more internal state words while pretending than when they're not pretending. (Hughes & Dunn, 1997) As well as children who engage more in pretend play use more emotional or internal state words compared to children who pretend less. (Howe, Petrakos, & Rinaldi, 1998) Meaning children who pretend can express more of an understanding of other's emotional states.

Furthermore, children who talk more about emotions tend to pass theory of mind tasks earlier than children who don't. (Dunn, Brown, & Beardsall, 1991)

Thus, all these findings suggest that role-play may provide a context for emotion-related learning. As well as it has been suggested that children's interest in people may influence their play styles and this may lead to earlier theory of mind development (Lillard, 1998).

This is supported even more by research that's showed so-called more 'difficult' children (I hate that term) like children who show antisocial behaviour tend to engage in more violent pretend play and they show relatively poor theory of mind skills. (Dunn & Hughes, 2001; Nelson et al., 2008)

On the whole, I think all this research has shown us how important pretend play is. I know what I'll be getting my children to do in the future!

Scaffolding and Play:

Casting our minds back to Vygotsky and his theory, he believed learning happens through scaffolding and this is a process of a more knowledgeable other helping a child solve a problem or achieve a goal that is cognitively beyond them.

A bit harsh but that's the theory.

Therefore, researchers have looked at the role of scaffolding in play.

This theory has been supported by research over the decades. For example, Nielsen & Christie (2008) found that children are more likely to produce new pretend acts after watching an adult engage in pretend to play with objects.

In addition, Haight & Miller (1993) did a very detailed and long study of pretend play with children were between 12 and 48 months, and they found that 75% of pretend play was, in fact, social, and not solitary.

In their study, the 'scaffolding role' was played by the parent or another knowledgeable other and in these scaffolding activities, at first, it seemed as if the child was being taught what to do during play. However, over time the children would take over the props, objects, and scenarios themselves.

On the whole, this suggests that scaffolding played a role in their ability to play.

Imaginary Friends or Companions:

Of all the stereotypical thoughts about children and play, the idea of imaginary friends has to be there.

Whilst, I didn't have an imaginary friend during my childhood, I always liked the idea and their portrayal on TV and in films.

Therefore, an imaginary friend is:

'a very vivid imaginary character that does not actually exist but is treated as real by the child, who plays with it and refers to it in conversation through the day' (Bouldin & Pratt, 1999, p. 400)

This was originally studied by early psychoanalytic theorists. Like, Green (1922) and Wickes (1927)

As well as the results of research in this area

suggests:

"the ideal means by which to study the nature and functioning of the psyche.... the way in which children use pretend companions to cope with internal and external demands mirror how the psyche later deals privately and personally with these elements" (see Klausen & Passman, 2007)

This is interesting because it shows that imaginary friends are logical and they help children to make sense of the very strange and complex social world around them.

Furthermore, imaginary companions are divided into 3 categories. Like, invisible characters and personified objects. For instance, when a child says that their teddy bear can talk and they can have tea parties with them.

Finally, you have children who engage in extended role-play with their imaginary friends by adopting alternative personas. Like, they're Batman or My Little Pony.

Personally, I had no idea My Little Pony was still a thing!

Also, according to Taylor et al (2004) 65% of children will develop an alternative persona by they're 8 years old.

Lastly, Roby & Kidd (2008) conducted a study on children's imaginary companions and they found that in a communication task children between 4 and

6 years with these alterative personas were more skilled at taking into account the information required when talking to an adult in a communication task.

CHAPTER 16: TECHNOLOGY AND FINAL NOTES

Later in the book, there's a whole section of the book dedicated to the topic of the media and how this affects children. Yet technology impacts how children play and develop so it's important we look at it now.

Personally, I never was much of a gamer during my childhood or adolescence but I did like assassin's creed and the lego games. So, there's only so much personal commentary I can add on this section.

Nonetheless, I want to add that there is a social side of gaming that there is hardly ever spoken about in the literature to some extent.

I found this social side rather useful because I had a friend a few years ago and we didn't see each other too much but it was always nice to play games with him and talk to him that way.

Anyway, there's a wide range of technology is available to children today. Including:

- Mobile phones
- Social media
- Online games
- Tablets
- Connected toys.
- Computer consoles
- Creative games. (like Minecraft)

However, this technology does have negatives and benefits.

To start off with the negative developmental outcomes technology can cause. Kuss & Griffiths (2012) found that a minority of internet game players experience symptoms that could be traditionally associated with substance-related addictions. For example, mood modification and an increase in the importance of the game to their lives, much like how drug users say drugs are important to them.

This links into the hotly debated topic of Gaming Disorders. Despite this still not being classified as a real thing in the Diagnostic manuals.

Additionally, Kuss et al (2014) reviewed 68 studies and they found that a number of core symptoms, like compulsive use as well as negative outcomes, that appear relevant for diagnosis with people who suffer from Internet addiction and other addictive disorders.

In other words, technology and the internet can lead to addiction and the same negative outcomes as drug addiction.

Moreover, Rikkers et al (2016) found a link between electronic gaming and mental health conditions as well as risk-taking behaviour in a sample of 3,000 11-17-year-olds.

Meaning playing video games can increase the risk of a child developing mental health conditions and an increase in risk-taking behaviour.

Well, I have to admit that was depressing reading.

<u>Cognitive Benefits:</u>

Moving onto the benefits of technology, Beavis et al. (2015) conducted a large survey of middle-school children, and they found that when gaming was involved, a connection between 'fun' and 'learning' was valued more where it occurred, and there was strong affirmation of the skills that games were good at teaching. For example, 'problem-solving' or 'making things interesting'

Another study of interest is Fokies (2017) that

compared different methods of teaching in 135 7-9-year-olds using conventional, board games or digital methods of teaching. The digital methods involved apps and tablets. The results showed the digital group outperformed the other two groups as well as the children rated their experiences as more positive.

Lastly, Hsin et al. (2014) analysed 87 studies on e-learning and technology. The results showed technology had positive effects on collaboration, interaction with others and multiculturalism.

Final Notes on Play:

Finally, research has shown children who perceive an activity as play tend to be more focused, attentive, motivated, and show signs of higher well-being while on the task (Howard & McInnes, 2013; Sawyer, 2017) As well as perceiving an activity as play creates an active engagement and enjoyment. This helps children to prepare the cognitive and emotional states to remain on-task and process information. (Lillard et al., 2011)

CHAPTER 17: WHAT IS DRAMATHERAPY?

Normally, I talk about psychotherapy or anything to do with clinical psychology in... Well, my clinical psychology or abnormal psychology books. But since dramatherapy is play focused, I might as well put this chapter in here.

Personally, I think dramatherapy is an interesting idea because it's modern and I think it's a fun alternative to the more traditional psychotherapies.

What is Dramatherapy?

Without you knowing what dramatherapy is, this chapter is pretty useless right?

Consequently, dramatherapy is a systematic psychological method that uses creativity and drama to explore a person's or a group's challenging circumstances. (Emunach, 1994) That combines psychotherapy, theatre and drama.

That was much more technical than I usually like but that's the best definition I could come up with.

Why Dramatherapy?

With there being over 200 different types of psychotherapy, why use dramatherapy?

Interestingly enough for me and people who like history, dramatherapy has its roots in Ancient Greece. Since in these times, the theatre was a source of public education, where debates about morality took place, and drama was used as a healing method (Brown, 1997).

Meaning when people engage with drama they can make use of their body through movement and their mind to engage with a new character.

As a fiction writer, I can see the parrel with fiction writing too because us writers get to engage with our own characters. Like, witches, detectives and more.

Sometimes it can be great fun!

Through this process, we can experiment with a new situation and we can use our imagination to come up with solutions regarding this situation (Brown, 1997).

Additionally, dramatherapy uses a range of dramatic as well as artistic methods to promote well-being, cultivate social and creative skills, and offer a deeper understanding of the different roles we can adopt in everyday life. For instance, we code adopt the roles of a mother, father, boyfriend, sister or many more. (Keder-Tahar & Felix-Kellermann, 1996)

In this therapy, there is a range of tools that the therapist and the client can use. Like, miming, body movement, play, poetry, sand play, role-play, improvisation, guided imagery, dance, music, story-telling and story-making, dolls and puppets, costumes, masks, makeup and drawing (Keder-Tahar & Felix-Kellermann, 1996; Landy, 2006)

If we link this to play then what dramatherapy is actually about is the use of symbolism and symbolic play to promote mental health and well-being.

How Does Dramatherapy Work?

The entire point of dramatherapy is to get the person to change the one area in their life that they're not happy with. This is done through the process of the particular art form used. Like, movements or role-play. And it is this art form that is the heart of this change. (Jennings, 1992).

Moreover, these processes allow people or members of a group to step outside their typical everyday reality and enter dramatic reality. Where they create and re-create their experience in a new and innovative way or ways.

Through these playful experiences, people can assess and understand their values, behaviours, relationships and many more. Including the rapid change of ineffective patterns of thought and behaviour. (Brown, 1997).

Therefore, by adopting a new character, this gives individuals a voice to thoughts and emotions they might have not otherwise been able to experience, as well as they can view themselves from a distance, just like spectators would do during a theatre play.

I want to give you a quick pause and comment on this so far. I know it seems far-fetched and definitely weird. But as a fiction writer, a creative person, I can see the logic behind it.

Also, if you think about the more traditional psychotherapies. Dramatherapy uses the same sort of ideas because you can still get in touch with yourself and your unconscious.

To me, this sounds like the psychodynamic approach.

Continuing on, this is the great paradox of drama therapy. Since you have the actual process of the art form used, like role-playing, and this creates a dramatic distance between the individual and self. This allows the person to recognise, appreciate, approach, as well as ultimately accept hidden and/or traumatised aspects of oneself, which otherwise would have stayed hidden from us. (Jennings, 1992).

Dramatic play:

Moving onto the different types of play involved in dramatherapy. The first type is dramatic play and this type allows play as well as drama to become a metaphorical 'as if' world. (Pitruzzella, 2004)

This is very important for a child's development because as Jenning (2015) explains:

"It is important that children have the opportunity to play 'distanced' roles, ie those that are in stories and plays. The paradox is that the child is likely to come nearer to their own experience than if they enact their specific, immediate situation"

Neuro-Dramatic Play:

Another type of play is called: Neuro-dramatic play and this has been used in dramatherapy, but it's important for child development too.

The theory behind this type of play was developed by Sue Jenning who is the pioneer behind the development of dramatherapy.

Furthermore, this type of play involves the earliest embodied experience in infants, starting from 6 months before birth and continuing until 6 months after birth. (Jennings, 2011, 2015)

In turn, this involves 'sensory, rhythmic and dramatic play' & influences the growth of healthy attachment.

This is particularly helpful for children who have experienced trauma.

Additionally, there are several types of neuro-dramatic play. Such as sensory play and messy play. This includes playing with finger paints, sticky dough and sand. This is useful to use with children who have experienced trauma as the mess helps them to express the mess and chaos of their feelings, and this allows them to eventually create some order in their lives.

Another type is rhythmic play. Like: drumming, clapping, dancing and singing. This allows children to rediscover a rhythm of their lives and many people who suffer from post-traumatic stress disorder (PTSD) need to rediscover their inner rhythm, which is often displaced in trauma.

Subsequently, you have dramatic play. For instance, interactive stories, monster-play as well as masks. This can help a child make sense of their awful experiences.

Also, monster-play helps children to overcome the feelings of helplessness associated with trauma. And the 'monster' can be the cause of the child's shame, blame and guilt, and fear. Becoming the monster is the first step to reducing its power!

EPR Paradigm:

In case, you're wondering how this works in the real world, Jennings (1998, 2013) created a developmental model of dramatic play called the EPR Paradigm. Which stands for Embodiment, Projection and Role.

Moreover, the model was based on their extensive observations of babies, children as well as pregnant women.

Interestingly, it follows the progression of dramatic play from the ages of birth to 7 years old.

Therefore, according to this model, the development of a child's dramatic play goes through 3 progressive phases.

In the first phase, the child uses embodiment play and focuses on physicality and neuro-dramatic play.

Next, the child progresses and starts to play with projections, the use of objects.

Finally, the child progresses to the last stage and the play becomes theatre. Also, this is a dramatic paradox because the child wants to be and doesn't want to be the theatre at the same time.

EPR Paradigm in Trauma:

In terms of trauma therapy, play involves both distanced roles in stories and play. As well as the paradox of drama. For example, '*I come closer by being more distanced*' (Jennings, 1998).

How to Play Out Distanced Roles in EPR:

If you ever end up using dramatherapy in play, then it might end up looking like this in a dramatherapy session with children who have experienced trauma.

Firstly, the therapists use large boxes and pieces of cloth to enable children to develop their own ideas and their own space.

Then the therapists would use simple roles with the children using single feelings. Like: you're the angry person. You might draw the faces of the people so the children can understand their emotions as well.

Afterwards, sometimes you might use an animal character that interacts with the children as it can be easier for children sometimes to create an animal world to talk about their own experiences.

Next, the children would use their favourite stories to interact with one another and a mask might be used as a starting point for the story. Since this allows children to experiment with different roles. For example, if you used a Zoro mask then the children could experiment with the roles of stretch, heroism, and leadership.

Finally, the therapists would use the ideas that have been created through the process of projective play, like the themes that emerge in their play sessions, to try and make more informed therapeutic decisions.

PART THREE: CULTURE, POVERTY AND TRAUMA

CHAPTER 18: CROSS-CULTURAL DEVELOPMENT

If you've read any other books from this series then you will know that I love culture and how it impacts our behaviour.

In fact, the majority of Social Psychology investigates how culture impacts our behaviour, as well as Abnormal Psychology, investigates how culture plays a role in developing and treating depression.

So, as you can see, I love culture.

However, how does culture affect our development?

Before, we even try to answer that question we need to first understand: what is culture?

What is Culture?

Our culture encompasses many things like knowledge, laws, beliefs, traditions, morals and values.

Also, culture can be defined as the collective ideals or products that exist as a whole unit as defined by a particular group at a particular time.

Geography and Ecology:

Interestingly, our geography and our ecology can have massive impacts upon our culture and by extension our development and we need to understand geography and ecology. So we can understand how our landscape affects us before this leads to cultural differences.

The reason for this is because human migration has caused people to live in many different environments, as well as societies progress- meaning settlements have moved from hunter-gatherers to agriculture.

This has other impacts on society as intensive farming leads to many social changes. For example, housing, population growth and division of labour.

As a result, new towns are formed, and new jobs emerge.

Furthermore, this intensive farming led to animals becoming domesticated, but this led to an increase in disease so immunizes were developed, evolved and passed onto the next generation.

Overall, the birth of agriculture led to people having to find new roles within society.

Yet this still doesn't explain why western and eastern cultures are so different?

Historical Background:

In countries like Greece, individual farms allowed a farmer to support their families. Whereas in the east, irrigation was difficult so people needed to work together to feed the community.

Also, these cultural differences can even be found in our philosophies.

Philosophical Differences:

For instance, Aristotle explained the world using objects. Such as the rock sank in the water due to the rock having the 'gravity' property as well as the wood floated in water because it had the power of 'levity' and Aristotle didn't mention the water.

Whereas, philosophy in the east saw actions through the field of forces. Like: the water. This allowed them to understand concepts like magnetism as well as tidal flow long before the west did.

Culture Shock:

As a lover of culture, I'm very interested in culture shock as it's a well-known phenomenon where people experience difficulties adapting and understanding a new culture.

Additionally, culture shock occurs in the following stages:

- Honeymoon- when you're amazed by this new culture and excited by it.
- Culture shock- the reality of cultural differences sink in and your struggle to adjust this new culture.
- Adjustment- you find new ways of adjusting to this culture.
- Mastering- you no longer struggle with this new culture.

Developing Cultural Differences:

Exploring this topic in more depth, we're going to have a look at the Kung people as Kung infancy is a famous example of cultural differences in psychology because of the Bakeman et al (1990) study.

The Kung people are largely hunter-gatherers with hunting missions often but on average adults only need to about 3 days a week.

I know what you're thinking- why don't we do

that!

On the other days, they spend their time in social contexts and their mobile life prevents them from gathering possessions.

Instead, objects are shared and valued as a community.

Hence, why this culture is collectivist in nature as they work collectively and they focus on the good of the group instead of the individual.

Please check out Social Psychology for more information.

Co-Sleeping:

Firstly, I want to give a bit of context about why we don't tend to do co-sleeping in the west. Despite there being many advantages to co-sleeping with a child.

Well, my university lecturer told us that co-sleeping has many benefits for the caregiver-child bond and to be honest, it is very safe and nobody dies from co-sleeping with their child.

But when it does happen and to the best of his knowledge, only 1 child has died from co-sleeping in the 2000s in the UK alone. The media explodes the story and persuades people how stupid and dangerous this co-sleeping is.

Although, this story and the campaign against co-sleeping is mainly pushed and sponsored by companies that make baby furniture for nurseries.

Consequently, you could probably say that society has been manipulated by these companies to think of co-sleeping as harming or killing your child.

As in the west, we tend to prepare a room for a newborn baby, but this isn't practised in 90% of countries.

Whereas, in many Asian countries mothers will lay next to their babies.

Some Supporting Studies Include:

- Whiting (1964) that studied 136 societies and found that 66% of societies share their beds with their babies and the majority of others share beds with parents.
- Burton and Whiting (1961) studied 100 societies and found that only American parents have a separate space for their babies.

Overall, co-sleeping is common in every country except western ones.

Motor Development:

Cross-cultural motor development differs between western as well as eastern societies because Ainsworth (1967) and Killbride and Killbride (1975) both found that Ghana babies walk earlier than western babies.

Nevertheless, those aren't the only studies to notice cultural differences in child development as Keller (2007) found a number of cultural and developmental differences between German and Cameroonians babies.

The reason for this difference is because the Cameroonians actively stimulate the muscles. Making their children able to walk soon than western infants that aren't stimulated.

I know what you're thinking- why would they try and make their child walk sooner as babies become hurricanes when they learn to walk?

It just goes to show the interesting differences between cultures.

Furthermore, Ainsworth also reported earlier development of language, social behaviour and grasping in the Cameroonian infants.

Yet these cultural differences are reflected in the culture's goals as well because the German culture had goals of creating babies that were psychologically autonomous, independent, self-assured and individual.

Whereas the Cameroonian goals were to create

babies that were interdependent, respectful, socially supportive and collectivist.

Another study that shows cultural differences in development is Lohaus et al (2008) as it found that Nso infants showed accelerated development compared to German infants. As at the age of three months 94.5% of Nso babies compared to 6.8% of German babies were sitting with support.

However, German babies developed language sooner.

Attachment:

Building upon what we're learnt in the attachment section, there are cultural differences between preferred attachment styles as well.

For example, the German culture values and it's common to observe the avoidant attachment type.

Whereas in the Israeli Kibbutz culture the most commonly observed attachment style is anxious ambivalent style.

Whereas in Japan and Dogon in West Africa no child shows the avoidant style.

Colour Perception:

Until Davidoff and colleagues conducted their research. It was commonly believed that colour perception is universal. Meaning that all cultures would identify dark red as dark red.

However, colour categorisation is strongly linked to the speaker's language.

One example of this cultural difference is that unlike English people, the Himba of Namibia don't distinguish between blue-green in terms of colour.

Yet they distinguish between colour boundaries that English speakers may not.

These findings are found in toddlers as well. Suggesting that this develops earlier in life.

<u>Spatial Cognition:</u>

This refers to how people think about positioning and spatial awareness.

For example, English speakers tend to use egocentric references, so where they are in reference to the object. Such as the man is to the left of the house.

Whereas, the majority of other languages tend to use allocentric references. These are object to object references. Such as the man's next to the bus stop or west of the house.

Additionally, research shows that 4-year-old children tend to use allocentric references then when they get to around 8 years old they move towards egocentric bias and use egocentric references.

CHAPTER 19: POVERTY

Poverty is the state of having no or little means to fulfil basic needs and as a result of that, a number of outcomes can arise that inhibit development.

Brooks and Dunn (1997) summarised that poverty has a number of key outcomes:

- Physical health as poverty leads to stunted growth, malnourishment and low birth weight.
- Lower cognitive ability
- Poorer school achievement
- Emotional as well as behavioural outcomes such as showing more aggression or fighting behaviour while feeling depressed or anxious on the inside.

The researchers suggested a number of pathways as well. These pathways are other factors that affect development in addition to family income.

- Availability of nutrition
- The physical condition of the home
- Amount of time parents spent with children
- Parenting style
- Punishment practices
- Parent's mental health
- Neighbour conditions
- And many more…

<u>Models of Poverty:</u>

There are two main models or theories that try to explain and predict the deciding factors in the argument of what factors affect development the most.

- The family stress theory states that the main variables that affect development are family-related. Like: parenting styles and communication strategies.
- The investment model states that the most important pathways that affect development are associated with real goods. Such as nutrition, opportunities to learn and enriched environments.

Personally, if you combine the two theories, I believe that you would be spot on and both are very true explanations of the factors that affect poverty-stricken people the most.

Pollitt (1995)

- Researchers carried out a study on four very poor villages in Central Guatemala over the course of 8 years.
- The participants were made up of over 2000 children and mothers.
- As protein was the main nutrient missing from the villager's diet. The villagers were given a nutrient supplement.
- Participants from two villages received a high protein supplement whereas the two other control villages got a supplement that contained far less protein.
- Results showed that a significant drop in infant mortality in both sets of villages, but with a 69% decrease in villages taking the high protein supplement compared to only a 24% decrease in the other two villages. Children on the lower protein supplement suffered a slower rate of growth and a slower rate of recovery from infection. They also learned to crawl and walk slightly later on average. Because these undernourished children remained small for their age, adults may have treated them as if they were younger than their actual age.
- In conclusion, this shows how poverty can affect psychological development.

Critical Thinking:

A positive of this study is that it has high ecological validity as the experiment uses a natural, real-world setting. In turn, this increases the generalizability of the findings, so we can apply the results of the experiment to different situations.

However, as a result of this high ecological validity where other factors that could influence cognitive development aren't controlled. We cannot say with unshakable certainty that protein was the only factor that could have given us these results. As factors could have potentially played a role. Like: illness, genetic factors and other missing nutrients from their diet.

CHAPTER 20: TRAUMA AND CHILDHOOD RESILENCE

Trauma is an emotionally painful experience that will have long-lasting effects on a person's development as well as well-being.

Deprivation is the continued exposure to negative circumstances.

Now both of these concepts are heavily linked as deprivation like poverty and other forms of deprivation can lead to trauma. Therefore, they are often studied together as they both have similar effects for development.

Effects of Deprivation in critical Periods:

Personally, I believe that language will be the easiest example to use here.

A critical period is the time in which a particular psychological function must be learnt in order for the function to develop properly.

The thinking is that if the function isn't developed in this critical period then it may never develop.

For example, speech must be learnt before the age of 5 otherwise it will never develop as supported by many case studies of individuals. Or at the very least you will never be fluent in a language.

This missing critical period could be down to:

- Abuse
- Malnutrition
- Living in silence
- Living in isolation
- And more…

There are many examples of these critical periods so I would encourage you to go online and try to find some examples.

Overall, if critical periods are missed then certain psychological functions may never develop.

Effects of Trauma:

Trauma can affect children in many ways, but the most common effect of trauma is the development or onset of Post-Traumatic Stress Disorder as demonstrated in the case study below. While it isn't on children. It still shows the effect trauma can have on people.

Additionally, NPY is called: Neuropeptide Y and it's a chemical in the body that causes people to overact and it increases in times of stress and trauma.

Morgan et al (2000)

- Researchers carried out a study on healthy US Army soldiers who participated in a survival course designed to match the conditions endured by prisoners of war. For example, they experienced food and sleep deprivation, isolation and intense interrogations.
- The 70 participants took part in the survival experience or the Prisoner of War experience.
- The participant's NPY levels; a chemical involved in a number of psychological and biological processes; were measured before the start of the training as well as after the conclusion of either the survival training or the Prison of War experience.
- The researchers found that NPY levels went up in the soldiers' blood within hours of the interrogations. They found a correlation between the soldiers' responses to the experience and their level of NPY. Those soldiers who responded more negatively to the training experience were those with lower levels of NPY.

Resilience:

Resilience is the ability to recover from negative events and adapt to stressful experiences.

Resilience is a key skill in life which allows us to be strong and cope with the world's hardships.

McFarlane (1983) demonstrated that a child's ability to show resilience depended on many factors including the resilience of their parents. Plus, the seriousness of the trauma didn't affect the resilience of the child as much as it affected their parents.

Betancourt et al (2013) demonstrated that former child soldiers were able to recover from the most traumatic of events, but they were shown the importance of social support in this process.

PART FOUR:
LANGUAGE
DEVELOPMENT

CHAPTER 21: INTRODUCTION TO LANGUAGE DEVELOPMENT

If you've read <u>Cognitive Psychology 2nd Edition</u> then you would know a bit about language, but it didn't investigate language from a developmental perspective as that is the focus of this book.

<u>Why is Language Important?</u>

Well, Language is important to learn. Due to if people struggle with language during childhood then these people can experience the following difficulties during adulthood:

- Significantly higher rates of anxiety disorder. (Beitchman, Wilson, Johnson, Atkinson, Young and Adlay, 2001)
- There's a relationship between language difficulties at the age of 5 and drug abuse as well as anti-social behaviour.

- Adults have social difficulties. Especially, if they have comprehension difficulties in primary school. (Howlin, Manvood and Rutter, 2000)
- Higher prevalence of communication disorders amongst male prisoners than the population as a whole. (Johnston and Hamilton, 1997)

How is Language Used?

Language is used in many different ways and language involves a lot of different components. Like: language comprehension; this refers to understanding what others say or what a sign said; and language production. This refers to actual speaking or signing to others.

In addition, language involves a lot of sub-components as well. Including:

- Phonology/ phonetics- the sound of the language
- Semantics- the system of decontextualized meaning
- Lexical item-words
- And more

And whilst, I explain and introduce what each of these sub-components are in Cognitive Psychology 2nd Edition. This chapter will almost exclusively look at how they develop.

Phonological Development:

A Phoneme is a difference in sound that is perceived by the speaker as discrete and distinguishing some words from another.

For example, k and g are phonemes. Resulting in kill and gill being two different words.

Also, whilst r/l are phonemes in English they aren't in Japanese.

This emphasises the importance of cross-cultural differences in development as shown in an earlier chapter.

In terms of development, we develop phonemes because at birth we are born with the ability to discriminate sounds of any language.

However, this ability declines during our first year of life. (Werker and Lalonde, 1998)

In more detail, phonemes develop across the lifespan in the following way:

- 0-2 months -Babies make a lot of non-communicative, nonspeech noises. Like: crying and fussing. This is universal across all cultures.
- 2-4 months- Cooing, more diverse vowels, beginning of syllables.

- 4-8 months- more obvious syllables- like units. (maaaa, mmmmmmmmma) This is where babies can produce a range of pheromones.
- 6-12 months- babies can perform Canonical babbling (Oller and Eilers, 1988) and real syllables.

Note: canonical babbling is; in essence; babbling that forms constants and vowels.

Then first words tend to happen about 12-15 months.

- 12-24 months- babies can perform complex babbling and some children use prosody.

Meaning that babies can create a range of complex phoneme.

Morphological Development:

Moving onto our next sub-component of language, a morpheme is the smallest meaningful unit of a word and at first, toddlers combine words omitting a lot of morphemes.

For example, a toddler may say 'he play tennis last week'

'yesterday I dance'

Although, the rate of omission gradually decreases by the age of 3 and a half, but if the omission continues by age 4 then it's a sign of language difficulties.

Learning to Generalise Regular Morphological Rules:

In many languages, morphemes with a certain meaning like past tenses may occur in regular or irregular forms.

Interestingly, it was only when I started to learn this topic that it occurred to me that English does have irregular verbs as I hadn't noticed these irregular verbs before as I just use them so regularly and easily without thinking.

Such as: ate instead of eated and ran instead of runed.

This links into the topic of overgeneration as children tend to treat irregular words as if they were regular before learning their correct spelling.

Syntactic Development:

The syntax is very useful in language as these are the rules which allow the organisation of words into large structures, and I elaborate more on the important and interesting nature of Syntax in Cognitive Psychology 2nd Edition- in case you wanted to know more.

One of the ways that Syntax is important is it allows us to use a finite set of words in our vocabulary and grammar and we can arrange and put together an infinite number of sentences and express an infinite number of ideas.

But how do we learn or develop an understanding of Syntax?

Between the ages of 12-18 months, we learn to understand simple sentences with familiar objects as well as actions were we have to calculate the relationship between the object and action.

Such as: "Pass me the keys," means that we need to understand the relationship between the object of the keys and the action of passing them to the speaker. Whilst the speaker pointed to the keys on the table.

Also, parents may help the child at this age by providing some structured support known as adult scaffolding.

Subsequently, at the ages of 18-24 months it is the same as before but this time there's no adult scaffolding to help the child understand.

Meaning no looking at the object or moving them as you speak.

Using our last example, at this age, the speaker would merely ask the child to pass them the keys instead of pointing.

Comprehension vs Production:

Comprehension is greater than production in typically and even atypically developing children, as well as at age 2 and onwards language comprehension can be a strong predictor of language development later on.

As if a child is not understanding simple phrases by 24 months he or she should be referred for assessment by a speech and language therapists.

Furthermore, by 5 years old, children have mastered the basic grammar of their native language. Whether this is spoken or manually signed.

Syntactic Production:

In English children begin to produce 'holophrases' These holophrases are entire phrases that are expressed in a single word. Like: "Howdy" for "How do you do?"

However, by 24 months, the majority of English-speaking children are producing at least two words combinations and this is described as telegraphic speech as nonessential elements are missing.

For instance:

- Read me- instead of Read to Me
- Tickle daddy- instead of Tickle me daddy.

Also, children love to ask lots of questions!

Subsequently, by 30 months, most children are starting to use a range of basic sentence types and imperatives.

Following this, children can start to learn how to form sentences as children gradually start to include more morphones to make full sentences.

For example, tickle me dad and read to me.

Thus, by four years, children should be proficient in the comprehension of a range of abstract semantic concepts. Such as: before, after, up and down. Using a range of connectives properly and they should have a comprehension of speech.

CHAPTER 22: THEORIES OF LANGUAGE DEVELOPMENT

Continuing our look at language, I want to look at a few extra theories of language development.

<u>Usage-Based Theories:</u>

Firstly, some researchers believe infants learn language, word meaning and syntax by learning mechanisms that are unique to humans. As well as it's important to note of these learning mechanisms are only used for learning language.

I think this makes sense because if other animals had the same learning mechanisms as humans. They would surely be able to speak English, Spanish, French, etc.

In addition, in usage-based theories, an infant's intention-reading and socio-cognitive skills can explain pragmatic development. For example, joint attention and theory of mind. Since an infant would need to be to able to understand the intention of others to be able to understand words to use in the social situation.

Furthermore, the theories emphasise the role of pattern/ statistical learning, this is where the infant can recognise the patterns in their language and judge the probability of a certain word being right for the situation, that's the user-friendly definition. As well as sufficient input is needed for word learning and syntax

Finally, joint attention is the shared focus of two people on an object. This occurs when one person indicates to the other person by glazing, pointing or any other verbal or non-verbal way of interacting to an object.

Overall, the theories argue socio-cognitive development is critical for word learning.

The Role of Input In Syntax Acquisition:

Building on from the last section, there's a lot of evidence to support the idea language input is important for syntax acquisition.

For example, there is a relationship between the degree to which a child's sentence comprehension improves. This happens around 42 to 50 months old and the percentage of multi-clause sentences they produce. (Huttenlocher, Vasilyeva, Cymerman & Levine, 2002)

Another way of putting this is the higher the language input, the better the syntax of the child.

Additionally, patterns in the language input can explain error patterns in a child's language (Rowland, Pine, Lieven & Theakston, 2005; Kirjavainen, Theakston & Lieven, 2009). For instance, if most of the input was wrong then the child would produce a lot of wrong language too.

However, there's evidence language input only plays a minimal role because infants show an early preference for word order with familiar words in their language. (Gervain et al., 2008)

Meaning once the child is familiar with words in their native language and that language's word order, the input matters very little.

Linguistic Nativist Theories of Word Learning:

The final set of theories we need to look at are Linguistic nativists. Unlike the usage-based theorists, these researchers believe we learn language using mechanisms that are only used for learning a language.

Meaning Linguistic nativists argue that human children could not learn word meanings and syntax without having innate learning mechanisms and innate representations specific to these domains.

These theories are made of up of two concepts.

The first concept is innate words and these are an infants learning biases or assumptions.

Secondly, you have the concept of the whole object assumption (Markman, 1991) This can be explained by when adults point to an object and say a word, the children assumes the word is the whole object and not a part or characteristic.

Another difference between the two types of theories are nativists believe syntax and lexical learning are separate processes using separate cognitive modules, as well as syntax learning is underpinned by underlying hierarchical rules universal to all language. (Chomsky, 1965, 1981, 1995)

Evidence:

Initially, the fact that Korean and Mandarin-speaking children use more verbs than English speaking children, in general, would seem to disprove the theory because this counters the whole object assumption. (Bloom et al, 1993; Gopnik & Choi, 1995)

In reality, even children learning languages, like mandarin and Japanese, which hear more verbs, because in these languages, nouns tend to be omitted more often show a tendency to map new words onto objects than actions. (Imai et al, 2005) This supports the whole object assumption.

A final piece of supporting evidence is the mutual exclusivity assumption. (Markman & Wachtel,

1988) This is the tendency for children to assume one word is used to one object. For instance, a cat is a cat and the term cat cannot be used to describe a dog.

CHAPTER 23: PRAGMATIC LANGUAGE AND WHAT INFLUENCES LANGUAGE DEVELOPMENT?

This refers to how language is used and interpreted in a contextualized and appropriate manner for the purpose of social interaction.

In other words, how we speak to people in social situations compared to speaking in a different situation. Like: a formal setting.

The two important aspects of pragmatic language is the Contextual appropriateness. This is where you adapt what you're saying to what your listener knowns, using the appropriate language register.

For example, I wouldn't start talking to you about publishing and the business of publishing how I would to an author friend, because it wouldn't be contextually appropriate. As chances are you don't know too much about the publishing industry.

And I would probably be the same about whatever industry you work in.

Subsequently, pragmatic language has a specific purpose to it. Such as: gossiping about the next-door neighbour's dog or relaying information about a great deal to your friend.

But how does Pragmatic language develop?

Pragmatic Development:

In all honesty, I have to confess that pragmatic language is very complex for the individual as it involves a lot of different skills. Like:

- Using the right words, slang or term to refer to something
- Understanding inferences.
- Being able to talk in different tones for different situations.

I know those skills sound very easy to us adults or teenagers but when you consider that 2-4-year-olds tend to refer to things in a way that's ambiguous to the person they're talking to. You can start to understand the difficulty.

For example, children tend to refer to something with pronouns even though the person they're talking to doesn't know who he or she is.

Such as, "He hit me today!"

Well, who's He?

As you can see the skills that are needed for pragmatic language get more complex and this is before you consider that children are often under informative up until to the ages of roughly 7 or 9. (Lloyd and Dahnhan, 1997, JPR)

Overall, pragmatic language is important for the social world, but it is complex as well.

However, it must be noted that there are key factors that can influence language development; including pragmatic language; as a whole.

Yet after all this talk about pragmatic language and more, what factors actually impact language development?

What Factors Can Affect Language Development?

Well, it turns out that a lot of different factors can and do influence a child's language development, but let's focus on a few key factors.

Therefore, two key factors that can influence language development are the quantity of language input to the child as well as the quality of language input to the child.

Quantity of Language Input:

One of the best ways to help a child speak is to talk in front of them and to them, but this is problematic as adults may differ hugely when talking to a child. In terms of words per hour, sentences per hour and sentence length when talking to a child.

Nonetheless, why is this quantity important for language development?

It's important because the variance in the quantity of language predicts a child's vocabulary development and processing speed. (Marchman &Frenald, 2008; Hurtado, Marchman and Fernald, 2008)

In other words, the higher the quantity of input to a child. The better vocabulary and processing speed they should have.

Finally, this is true for teachers and children in the classroom as well. (Huttnlocho, Vasilyeva, Cynerman and Levine, 2002)

Quality of Language Input:

Although, there must be high quality in language input as well as a high quantity of language input.

One of the main reasons why quality is important is because the lack of quality in language input can explain the variance in a child's poor language development that is usually attributed to a child's poor socioeconomic status.

Nonetheless, another main and extremely important reason why quality is important is that the role of interaction with a child must be interpersonal.

I mean if you merely put a child in front of a TV; a possibly higher quantity of language input; then the child will still struggle with language development.

As Roseberry, H Hirsh-Pasek, Parish-Morris and Golinkoff (2009) found that only if someone is live sitting beside a child describing the TV can a child learn from a TV.

Cognitive Brain Systems Involved in Language Development:

As a quick final section on language development, I wanted to quickly mention that a lot of different brain systems are involved in language. For instance,

- Auditory and visual system as you need to match what you hear to what you see
- Memory system as you need to remember what you've learned and seen
- Attention system- pay attention to what people are saying
- Processing system- link words to meaning
- Inferencing system- interpret the message

Parting Note:

We cannot forget that human communication is a two-way street so it partially relies on the child's socio-cognitive skills as well.

PART FIVE: SENSORY DEVELOPMENT

CHAPTER 24: SENSORY DEVELOPMENT AND THE DEVELOPMENT OF VISION

Moving onto our last section in this developmental psychology book, we'll focus on how we develop our senses and perceptions.

If you want to learn about this topic from a biological standpoint then please see Biological Psychology 3rd Edition for more information.

Firstly, we can understand the origins of the biological structures that our senses develop from in terms of Phylogeny; this covers the evolutionary origins of a species; and Ontogeny. The developmental lifespan of a single organism

In addition, after conception and around the 10-26 week mark, the rate of brain growth is around 250,000 cells a minute. (Covan, 1979)

Note: the comment or assumption that the

human eyes do not grow is a MYTH.

The Development of The Senses:

Over the next few sections, we'll be focusing on and explaining how the different senses develop.

As we focus on the developmental side of the senses in this chapter, I would encourage you to read the Sensory Section of Biological Psychology 3rd Edition as a companion guide to this book.

Auditory senses:

Interestingly, babies are capable of hearing after 19 weeks of conception (Heppper & Shahidullah, 1994) as amniotic fluid in the ear cannel attenuates auditory response, as well as fetal hearing, occurs via bone conduction.

Taste:

This sense is particularly difficult to measure in infants as we can't simply ask them how did something taste and did they like it.

Meaning that we need to use other methods and facial expressions to help us understand if infants are sensitive to different tastes. Such as an infant's muscles relax when they taste something sweet. (Steiner, 1979)

This is important for survival as bitter food could

be toxic and thus kill the infant.

On the other hand, if an infant dislikes a particular taste then they can begin to like the taste if it's given to them at times of hunger.

Smell:

Our ability to smell is an extremely important sense as it allows us to smell toxins in the air and it allows us to find food.

In terms of development, infants show an odour preference at birth as well as the smell of rotten food makes a baby frown. (Steiner, 1979)

Touch:

For infants, touching; which is well developed at birth; is a fundamental way to interact and it helps to build bonds with the infant and caregiver or anyone else.

Additionally, babies respond positively to touch as it can cause them to smile and pay attention (Stack & Muir, 1992)

Although, how do infants develop movement and reflexes?

<u>Reflexes and Motor Development:</u>

A reflex is an automatic reaction without conscious thought and new-born babies are born with a number of reflexes, each with their own unique purpose and survival value:

- Blinking- protection
- Rotting and sucking- nursing
- Stepping and crawling- early component of locomotion
- Move and Grasping- likely to have been functional in earlier stages of evolution and is used for gripping the mother.

Interestingly, most of a baby's reflexes disappear by the age of 6 months and eye blinking is the only reflex that exists throughout the human lifespan.

The reason this happens is because reflexes are phased out as the behaviour becomes more voluntarily controlled through the development of the cerebral cortex.

In addition, it's important to test reflexes in babies and children because if reflexes persist then it could mean that the cerebral cortex is damaged. Equally, an absent or a number of weak reflexes can tell us about the central nervous system's working.

Gross Motor and Fine Motor Development:

Just to clarify because I doubt many people know what gross and fine motor skills are. I know I didn't until I started to write this book.

- Gross motor skills are movements that involve the whole body. Like: moving your arm.
- Fine motor skills are movements that involve the movement of small muscles. Like: moving a finger and not the whole hand.

Developmentally speaking, there are two ways how movement develops. The ways are Cephalocaudal. This is head to tail development where you develop head control first.

Then you have Proximodistal control. This refers to centre- outwards development. Like you can control your arm before you can control your finger.

However, we haven't spoken about how vision develops, so I wonder how our vision develops?

Visual Development

Whilst my personal interest in developmental psychology might be limited and I certainly wouldn't go into the field for a career. I have to admit vision is an interesting area in my opinion.

So, throughout the chapter, we're going to

explore the differences between adult and infant vision.

Background Information:

There are many differences between infant and adult vision but to give you some general ideas about the differences I want to give you some information.

Consequently, in the eye, there are cells called cones. These are specialised cones that are light sensitive and very important for colour vision.

In adults, cones are packed into a part of the eye called the fovea, but in infants, cones are evenly distributed in the eye.

Another difference is in infants there near sight is blurry whereas an adult's near sight is relatively clear.

Of course, it depends on how close you hold an object!

Interestingly, an infant's visual system is anatomically there but it's immature and it needs to develop in a few ways.

For instance, it isn't possible for infants to perform coordinated eye movements, as well as an infant's eye movements are relentless. Compared to adults, which only perform 2 to 3 eye movements per second.

Development of Visual Orienting:

This is the first major area of visual development, we'll look at because orienting ourselves to our environment is important.

Therefore, visual activity is highest in the fovea, and a saccade, a quick rapid movement of the eye, points the fovea to areas of interest. This brings the area into focus.

However, New-borns cannot make reliable saccadic movements. Resulting in them making errors and sometimes they produce saccades in steps. (Askin & Salaptek, 1975)

On the whole, eye movements in infants are slow and inaccurate but these become more focused by 2 months old and near adult-like by 4 to 6 months. (slater, 2001)

Although, infants are able to perform eye movements to track an object and from birth, new-borns can scan the environment from objects of interest as well as track moving ones. Like: an adult walking towards them.

They scan their environment in the first few days of life. Haityh (1980) when the researchers found when they're are in a darker room., new-borns showed short eye movements. These are called: endogenous eye movements. Also, they respond to stimulation from the environment as well. An example of exogenous eye movements.

Depth Perception:

This type of perception can be defined as having the visual ability to be able to perceive the world as 3 dimensional, and this is important for reaching as well as understanding the environment.

Also, having a sensitivity to depth allows the infant to explore the environment safely. Since I can imagine the terrible situation of an infant not being able to understand there's a small ten centimetre drop when they're crawling about.

Interestingly enough, infants as young as 4 months have some sense of depth because they can fixate on targets at different distances and track objects moving in depth. (Hainline & Riddel, 1995)

But the really interesting thing about human vision is sometimes our brain cannot understand depth because of binocular disparity. This is where there are different images coming into each eye.

Kinetic Depth Cues:

Lastly, these depth cues involve tracking the movement of bodies or objects and 3 to 4 week olds blink defensively as objects come towards their eyes. (Nanez & Yonas, 1994) as well as this can be understood by the Maton Parallax. This is where close objects move more than distal objects when you are in motion or stationary. This is can be observed in infants as earlier as 16 weeks and beyond.

Development Of Vision

As the importance of vision is pretty clear, I think we can skip an introduction to this section.

Therefore, at birth babies have a pretty basic visual system because they have everything that an adult has, but some of the vision systems are still immature in its first year.

For example, the lens often over and under accommodate objects. This means that it is sometimes difficult to focus on objects.

On the other hand, some developments to the visual system happen across childhood as well. (Hainline, 1998)

How Strong Is An Infant's Vision?

We know adult eyesight is tested by getting an adult to read lines off a Snellen chart.

However, babies can't do this so instead they use the preferential looking method. (Fantz, 1964; Dobson and teller, 1978; Atkinson, 2000)

In addition, within hours of being born new-born babies have a prenatal fixation on the mother's face. (Field et al, 1984)

Moreover, at only two days old a baby can distinguish between emotional expressions. This is important for socio-emotional development. (Field et al, 1983)

This evidence suggests that a baby's ability to see shapes depends on innate mechanisms or mechanisms in the visual system that are fine-tuned without much experience needed after birth. (Morton and Johnstone, 1991)

Although, animal research has shown that innate characteristics of the visual system can be undone by environmental factors. If the environment isn't visually stimulating enough.

In other words, a baby can tell the difference between emotional expressions because they have been born with the ability to do so.

When Can Babies See Colours?

Whilst, the research on infants and colour vision is more contentious. The current view is that babies have at least some version of colour vision and this vision rapidly develops in the first few months of their life, and we can measure this using a range of different methods.

Additionally, focusing on the biological side, by

the age of 1-2 months we know that babies do have the equipment or apparatus in their visual system to be able to see colours.

Although, the development of seeing bluish colours may come later. (Knoblauch et al, 1998; Adams and Courage, 2002)

The theory behind this is that babies prefer to look at something rather than nothing. Resulting in the baby being shown a pattern of black and white stripes and a blank white sheet.

Therefore, the baby will look at the stripes and the stripes get thinner and thinner until the babies show no preferences. That's the limit of the baby's vision.

Equally, a more sophisticated method is achieved by using: visually evoked potentials. (VEP) or EEG that measures a baby's brain waves during the activity.

The result shows that a new-born's vision is about 20/600 so a new-born can see what an average adult can see at 600 feet but this rapidly improves to 20/60 by 6 months to 20/20 vision by 9 months.

Other Colour Vision Time Marks:

By 3-4 months- babies can perceive all four basic colours and hues as adults do. These hues are red, blue, yellow and green. (Hainline, 1998; Teller, 1998; Teller and Bornstein, 1987) as well as colour vision seems to be an innate factor, ability or process that mature later on.

Regardless of the correct answer, the baby's environment must be stimulating in infancy to be sustained. Because Sugita (2004) showed that young monkeys can lose their natural colour vision if they're raised in an environment with limited colours.

Do Babies See A Coherent World?

This question has been answered using the preferential looking method as well as the research method of habituation and familiarisation. This is a process of constantly showing a baby an object until the baby gets bored and then you show them a new novel object to see if their interest increases. If it does then you know that baby can tell the difference between one object and another one.

Although, do babies coherently see shapes?

It turns out that new-born babies do as they show a preference for certain shapes and they have a great bias towards facial shapes. (Dannemiller and Stephen; Leo and Simon 2009)

Consequently, both of these methods and research findings show that babies do coherently see the world.

A Quick Introduction to Infant perception:

We experience sensations on a daily basis whether it be through touch, taste or vision. We experience the world, but how do we develop these sensory systems and others?

Firstly, we can define sensations as the processing of inputs that we get from sensory organs like the eyes, skin and ears, receiving stimuli from the external world.

Interestingly, decades of modern research like Slater and Lewis (2002) have shown that earlier views were wrong about the development of perception.

This is because through refinement from childhood to adulthood. A child's senses are largely as good as an adult's sense.

Parting Note:

I truly hope that you have enjoyed these two chapters and this book and as we have focused on the developmental side of the senses in this chapter, I would encourage that you to read the Sensory Section of Biological Psychology as a companion guide to this book.

CHAPTER 25: COGNITIVE DEVELOPMENT OF FACIAL PROCESSING

When I first knew this lecture was going to be taught in my child development module, I was disappointed and I thought this was going to be a very boring topic. Yet I have to admit it is interesting and worth looking at.

So, humans are a species of primates, not surprising and like most primates love being a part of social groups.

The downside of being in social groups is the existence of a large social group involves the identification of individuals and assigning them a social status.

Consequently, it's important for us to be able to reliably categorise and individuate people we encounter.

Why Faces Are Important?

As I preluded to in the section above, faces are important because they share a lot of information about the person they're attached to. (There's no better way to put it, sorry) Such as age, gender, expression and more.

Additionally, facial recognition is important for survival, judging fertility (Jones et al, 2005), assessing group status and recognising individuals.

Cross-Species Face Recognition:

It turns out there are similarities in the facial processing systems of different species. As a result of many primates have a preference for the face of their own kind. (Kin, Gunderson & Swartz, 1999) and some researchers have suggested it might reflect a common origin selected by evolution. (Pascails & Kelley, 2009)

Theoretical Accounts of Face Recognition:

Whilst, we might not know for certain how humans process faces, I have always appreciated and admired how some people have thought about how we do this special type of processing.

One such account is the Bruce and Young Model (1986) and this proposes our recognition is facilitated by the development of Person identity Nodes (PIN) which are composed of Face recognition Units. (FRN)

Then we manage to identify familiar faces through the activation of stable average representation. (Valentine, 1991)

A much better way to put this model is we recognise familiar faces because we remember the unique facial features of the individual and we can detect these features. Due to we know what an average human face should look like.

Cortical and Neural Basis of Face Recognition:

The brain is heavily influenced in our processing of faces because the brain area known as the Fusiform Face Area is activated by faces more than any other object. As well as if a brain lesion develops in this area it results in prosopagnosia. (face blindness)

Suggesting it's vital for face processing.

Additionally, since there are many aspects to face processing, including detection and recognition, it has been suggested face processing involves a distributed network of regions.

Similarities have been found amongst other species.

Overall, this suggests that face processing

involves an evolved network of brain areas.

Face Detection:

Using a technique that is used by several authors called the visual array, we are able to study face detection since we know faces are found efficiently when they're displayed in a grid. (Jacobsen et al, 2016)

Also, studies show adults are faster at detecting human faces than non-human faces.

All in all, we can effectively study face detection and humans are very good at it.

Therefore, there's a theory called the 'Two Process Theory of Face Processing' that aims to explain it in further detail.

This is a popular development theory that suggests humans have subcortical (CONSPEC) and a cortical system (CONLERN) for face detection.

The theory proposes that the subcortical system detects faces and it guides our visual attention towards the relevant stimuli.

Originally, researchers considered the subcortical system to decline after 1 month of age. (Morton & Johnson, 1991) but modern development psychologists acknowledged face detection continues into adulthood.

In case, you're confused. I am too. I don't understand why they thought face detection stops at 1 year old. What happens when you go into school or the workplace? Are there no new faces to detect?

Also, whilst the theory suggests eye contact may be critical for face processing (John et al, 2015) findings from Kelley et al (2019) suggest that may not be necessary.

Although, the findings of these studies might be down to stimuli and the methods used.

Additionally, early in life infants can detect individuals private faces. (Pascails, de Haan & Nelson, 2002) and this reflects the plasticity of infant face processing. I do enjoy the topic of neuroplasticity, Biological Psychology.

However, this ability does decline between 6-9 months of age unless artificial exposure is provided. (Pascails et al, 2005)

Vision and Race:

When I was researching this book, I came across a few sources saying stereotypes impact our vision and if we link this to infant vision, research has found new-borns can perceive differences in racial categories but it's meaningless to them.

Yet if infants are predominantly exposed to own-race faces they develop a preferential looking by age of 3 months. But that could be undone since another race face could be deemed novel for infants, and we know infants are interested in novel objects and people.

Overall, this emphasises how early facial processing is influenced by the environment.

Perceptual Narrowing:

This is where the brain uses our environmental experience to improve our perception and our facial preferences become 'tuned' by environment sensory input.

For example, an infants preference for their mother's face at 3 days of age. (Buschnell et al, 1989)

What Is the Function Of Narrowing?

Developmental psychology isn't certain what narrowing does but its probable that narrowing helps us to become more efficient at processing the types of information most frequently encountered. Like, it improves our processing of our family because we tend to see them more often.

Also, this is a reflection of the interaction between the infant's immature cognitive systems and their early experience. They both develop and improve over time.

Early Visual Deprivation:

We know that adult level of vision takes years to develop. (Larey & Diamond, 1994) and adults show sensitivity to spatial configuration of facial features configural processing.

In other words, adults are sensitive to facial looking objects.

However, Le Grand et al (2001) found that deprivation of pattern visual information left permeant deficits in configural processing.

Meaning if infants get a lack of pattern stimuli, this will leave deficits in their visual processing forever.

Knowing What Others Know:

When adults are talking to infants about unfamiliar or new objects like keys, children know adults know the label of a familiar object, like the word key, so the child can assume (using intention reading) that the adult intends the new object when the adult asks the child to show them the object.

PART SIX:
DEVELOPMENT OF
PROSOCIAL
BEHAVIOUR

CHAPTER 26: INTRODUCTION TO THE DEVELOPMENT OF PROSOCIAL BEHAVIOUR

When I was deciding what to write about this chapter, I struggled between putting this chapter in this book or Psychology of Relationships. But this chapter focuses on how Prosocial behaviour develops in children. So, it had to go in this book.

Prosocial behaviour is all about behaviour that helps and benefits others.

Another definition is:

"Any voluntary, intentional action that produces a positive or beneficial outcome for the recipient, regardless of whether that action is costly to the donor, neutral in its impact, or beneficial."

This includes any helpful action or behaviour that benefits others without it necessarily providing any direct benefits to the helper. As well as Prosocial behaviour is the opposite of antisocial behaviour.

4 Forms of Prosocial Behaviour:

In total, there are four types of Prosocial behaviour that people can show.

Firstly, there's instrumental or helping behaviour. This involves supporting other people to help them reach their goals.

For example, I like to think I'm showing this type of behaviour by writing this book and hopefully you learning this information will help reach your goals whatever they may be.

Equally, you're showing this behaviour towards me because by buying this book you are supporting me as an author.

Secondly, you have informing others. This involves sharing useful information with other people.

For instance, you may give people directions and this is what I do on The Psychology World Podcast.

Another type of Prosocial behaviour is comforting others. Also known as emotional support. Since you aren't directly getting anything from them. Except from being a great person.

The final type of Prosocial behaviour is sharing. This can be described as sacrificing your own resources.

Regardless of the type of Prosocial behaviour is used, 18-month infants help others achieve their goals. (Warneken & Tomasello, 2006)

Warneken & Tomasello, 2006

The researchers presented 24 18- month-old infants with 10 different situations were an experimenter was having trouble achieving their goal in 4 scenarios. Their problem could be as simple as an adult dropping something, or a situation where an adult struggles to open the door.

In the study, the infants were placed in a room where they could walk into the fallen object or they had to climb over quite a few obstacles for them to reach the desired object, in order to help.

The researchers found no difference between the infants who had to walk into the item very easily and those who had to struggle to get to the experimenter.

Regardless of the situation, the infants helped the experimenter even if they had to leave the toy they were playing happily with.

Which if you've seen infants playing with toys then you know how annoyed they get when you interrupt them!

In another study, the researchers redid the experiment with rewards for helping and their results weren't different.

Again, the infants helped regardless if they got a reward or not.

Some other results from the experiment showed that the helping behaviour wasn't influenced by parental presence or encouragement, and the children helped regardless of being rewarded or whether the helping is costly.

In another scenario, children were given a similar scenario where an adult drops an item.

However, in this case, the experimenters drop multiple objects which they couldn't reach. Meaning, they could not finish what they were doing.

Then to add yet another interesting twist half of the objects were relevant to the task the researcher was doing and the other half were irrelevant to the task. For example, if an experimenter was writing with a pen, and he dropped his pen, 5 pence, and a cloth. The idea is if the child wanted to help the researcher, they would pick up the pen and not the irrelevant objects.

Personally, I think this is a bit difficult considering the cognitive structures involved.

However, amazingly this is what they found. The child would pick up the pen and give it to them. If the experimenter was hanging clothes, the children would give him the cloth peg.

In the second experiment, the researchers investigated whether children's arousal was triggered by a social motive to see others being helped appropriately.

In other words, the researchers wanted to see if children enjoyed seeing others helping people.

Therefore, the researchers created a situation that was witnessed by the children.

Again, the researchers used the same sequence as before. So, an adult drops an item and then they drop an irrelevant item.

What's different is there's a social situation in which a helper is there to help the child. This is another adult.

Or if the adult helper wasn't there, the researchers created a situation in which the item flew to the adult by magic. This was known as the non-social situation.

The idea being if the satisfaction was about the order of things, children would be equally satisfied whether another person helps or the object flies back on its own, by magic.

(Yes, I can't believe they're describing it like that)

Interestingly, what the researchers found is if the adult helper gave the adult the irrelevant object instead of the one the adult was using. The children's arousal level increased. This indicated to the researchers that they wanted the experimenter to have their item back, the one he needed.

Whereas if there was no helper involved in non-social condition and the irrelevant item was returned by magic, then there was no arousal.

In other words, children reacted only in a social situation and this is where they wanted to help.

Personally, I can imagine their arousal increasing because of the great thing about children is they love to help.

God, I remember when my nephew (a 2-year-old) use to grab the broom and help clean. That was funny!

Overall, from these studies, we know children like to help out.

CHAPTER 27: TODDLER HELPING BEHAVIOUR AND SHARING

Do Toddlers Help A Peer?

So far we've looked at preschoolers and other infants with their prosocial behaviour. But now we need to look at how toddlers help. Since these infants are more able to help because they can talk and talk.

Therefore, toddlers' skills and motivations of helping do not depend on having a competent and helpful recipient, such as an adult, but rather they are much more flexible and general. (Hepach et al, 2016)

Information:

For the first type of prosocial behaviour, we'll look at sharing information because this is the easiest form of sharing. As well as toddlers do naturally point at things.

They tend to do this for two main reasons.

Firstly, infants point to effectively order an adult to do something for them. Like: give them juice!

Or infants can point declaratively when they want an adult to share attention with them to some interesting event or object.

But are they informative?

At 12 months of age, infants point towards the object that another person is looking for. (Liszkowski et al, 2006)

Overall, the answer is yes toddlers can share information and help others.

Comforting:

The next form of prosocial behaviour is comforting. This is a bit more difficult because it sympathy, feeling concern for others, and empathy. This involves feeling how the other person feels and being able to put yourself in their shoes.

Overall, comforting develops gradually because if we put a calm baby next to a crying baby. Then at first, the baby will start to cry as this is personal distress.

I can understand why. The baby is distressed by the other child!

Meaning they don't show sympathy, but this is a primitive response of empathy.

Then we have emotional contagion; this involves infants younger than 18-months; in this case, they witness another child cry but this time they cry in sympathy for the other child. Yet at this time, the infants cannot differentiate yet between their own feelings and another baby's.

By 18 months the infants start separating their feelings and others. Consequently, when another baby cries, they don't cry with the other baby but they try to comfort them the same way they would be comforted themselves. For example, if when they cry their mum holds them, they will allow their mum to hold the crying infant.

This is important when we remember how, for lack of a better term, possessive babies can be when it comes to their caregivers.

By 3- years, they are more competent in providing the right kind of comfort.

On the other hand, Dunfield et al when they examined the ability of 18- and 24-month-old infants to engage in helping, sharing, and comforting behaviour. The researchers found that the infants didn't do anything. They froze. None of the infants in either of the groups verbally reassured, questioned the injured experimenter or approached her to provide physical reassurance.

Do Young Children Sympathize Less In Response To Unjustified Emotional Distress?

Unlike adults or older children, a 3-year-old child's sympathy and acts of prosocial behaviour are not automatic responses. Instead, these processes involve taking into account whether the displayed distress is justified. (Hepach et al, 2012)

Also, I might as well add this is the same for adults in some situations because I know of times when I am less likely to give people a lot of sympathy if they don't deserve it.

On the other hand, at 2 years old, children proactively remedy unintentional accidents.

<u>Do Infants Have A Concept Of Fairness?</u>

I ask this question because sharing, one of the four types of prosocial behaviour, involves an understanding of fairness and distributive justice.

Interestingly, children seem to understand fairness because preverbal infants expect goods to be allocated equally, as well as they expect people to distribute goods equally and infants prefer fair over unfair distributors of goods. (Schmidt 2011; Geraci 2011; Meristo 2012; Sloane 2012; Sommerville 2013)

So, if you want infants to like you, you better be fair!

<u>Do Children Choose Or Prefer To Share With</u>

Others?

This depends because in choice tasks 3-year-olds prefer to share with others. Yet if the choices are costly, they don't prefer to share until 5 to 8 years old.

However, when children play dictator games based on economic theory. Young children usually keep to the majority to themselves. Until they are 5-9 years old when they start to share more equally.

CHAPTER 28: TAKE HOME MESSAGE, FINETUNING FACTORS AND PROSOCIAL BEHAVIOUR IN OTHER SPECIES

Take Home Message:

Overall, children show a wide range of positive social behaviours early on in life, and it seems humans have a genuine concern for the welfare of others.

Thankfully, prosocial behaviour doesn't depend on knowing the concept of helping or even knowing that you're helping. Nor does it matter if the recipient, like an adult, is helpful.

Instead, prosocial behaviour is a lot more flexible and generalised.

Finetuning Factors:

There are several factors that influence helping behaviour in children and adults for that matter. I talk more about these factors in <u>Social Psychology</u> and <u>Psychology of Relationships</u>, but I thought I would mention them here.

In terms of helping behaviour, who's fault it is, the competence, moral dilemmas, Bystanderism all influences whether or not the child (or adult) will help.

For sharing behaviour, the value of the resources, the ownership, merit, understanding of the resource and who needs the resources more all influences whether sharing will occur.

This makes sense because if we need the resources more than the other person or the resources are extremely valuable, like gold, than we are less likely to share them.

Whereas for comforting behaviour, the factors of who's fault it is, their age, the responsibility and kind of damage influences this behaviour. Since we're much less likely to comfort someone if it's their own fault or if the damage is minor.

Is Prosocial Behaviour Unique To Humans?

To complete this part of the book looking at prosocial behaviour, we need to talk about if humans are special in the fact, we can show prosocial behaviour.

Interestingly enough, the answer isn't as straight forward as you might think because chimps do pick up dropped objects, and chimps have similar tendencies to infants. Yet the helping they show is less flexible and robust.

Also, chimps do perform well in reaching tasks, like reaching something to help out an adult, but they don't perform well in other helping tasks.

Then you have some methodological issues. Like the experiments in this area uses a familiar keeper that rewards the chimps. So, is it helping or doing something for a reward?

As well as it is difficult to find chimps in the wild helping each other.

In short, they do help but not as robustly as human children.

Continuing with this section, chimps don't inform others, one of the four types of prosocial behaviours, and only chimps raised in captivity point to things.

Additionally, chimps' intentions aren't for helping, they are mostly to get objects and actions, like feeding. Also known as acquisitive motivation.

However, chimps do comfort each other and they have the potential for empathy. As well as consoling behaviour has been observed in wild chimps. Like: kissing, embrace, touch, play and grooming.

This is linked to reducing the stress of victims after aggressive attacks out of sympathetic concern.

Moving onto our last type of prosocial behaviour, chimps don't share and they only engage in 'passive' sharing. Like: the pressure of harassment over food quality and too big to monopolise.

In other words, they are effectively bullied into sharing.

Also, the dominant chimp gets the most resources and chimps do not show an inequity aversion.

Leading us to ask:

Is Prosocial Behaviour Intrinsically Motivated?

In a way, the answer is yes because there is an inborn motivation to form cooperative relationships with others, and we know strategies for reaching out to others in the spirit of mutual trust.

Along with children show spontaneous prosocial behaviour without the need for prompting or asking as well as there are universal prosocial qualities in all cultures.

In other words, yes. Prosocial behaviour is innately found in children.

PART SEVEN: CHILDERN AND THE MEDIA

DEVELOPMENTAL PSYCHOLOGY

CHAPTER 29: INTRODUCTION TO THE MEDIA

I think it's fair to say we all know about the debate surrounding whether screens and technology are bad for children.

As much as I would love to give you an answer, I cannot since professional opinions are mixed.

All I can do is talk about the research in this chapter and say you might want to look at Cognitive Psychology. Since there's a chapter that goes into the positives and negatives of technology on our mental processes.

Statistics:

Over 80% of US pre-schoolers watch TV every day. (Sesame Workshop, 2009) and children aged between 2 to 5 years old watch more than 3.5 hours of TV a day.

In the UK, children tend to spend 3 hours a day on the internet, 2.1 hours watching TV and YouTube is the most popular source of entertainment for children, with 61% of children watching YouTube daily.

Plus, there has been a decrease in reading over the years.

Source: Childwise Monitor.

But as an author and a person who keeps a very close eye on the book industry, I think that statistic is false and the children book market continues to grow.

As well as the eBook market and the audiobook market are booming. Including children's audiobooks and eBooks.

Also, I think this is a very misleading statistic that only incorporates some of the data.

Finally, I doubt that stats takes independently published books into account as these publishers and authors dominant the children's book market.

That's the short version.

<u>Media Types:</u>

As you can probably guess, children are exposed to a lot of different types of media. For example, Screen media. This includes:

- TV
- Film
- YouTube
- Apps
- Video games
- Ebook

Then books and podcasts are other forms of media children are exposed to.

Speaking of podcasts, if you don't want to buy Cognitive Psychology, if you go to episode 1 of The Psychology World Podcast, I talk about the pros and cons of technology on our mental processes there.

Do Children Learn From Screen Media?

This is the big question, isn't it?

It's all well and good saying children can or can't learn from screens, but we need to follow the research.

However, this isn't straight forward because there are a lot of factors to consider. Like: the child's age, their family and their socioeconomic status, their social context and individual characteristics. Those were all examples of child-level factors.

Nonetheless, the type of media can impact a child' ability or inability to learn from media. Such as the type of media, the pace of the media as well as the content.

Due to children are going to learn more from engaging age-appropriate content compared to a TED talk on biological psychology.

Additionally, environmental factors impact learning from media because the type of exposure an infant has, and the presence or lack of a caregiver influence the results too.

Finally, the rest of the section as we're looking at the research on this area, we need to focus on the child's language, executive functions, academic performance, literacy and numeracy skills and prosocial behaviour outcomes.

But can children learn from Video?

CHAPTER 30: CAN CHILDERN LEARN FROM VIDEO?

Young Children and Video

Diving into this topic in more depth, the short answer is no young children cannot learn from video.

One possible reason is because the video content often gives an inaccurate representation of the real world. But even when the video is realistic young children still have trouble learning from the video.

For example, videos are perfectly polished, so the viewer rarely gets to see what it's really like in the real world where it's recorded.

Does Screen Media Affect Language?

Since the studies explain the range of interesting results about this topic, it's better if we just dive into them.

Learning from Video: Infants

Robb, Richert & Wartella (2009) researched 12 to 15-month-old infants who watched a DVD that was designed for word learning for 6 weeks. Their results showed word learning didn't have an increase in their language abilities.

More specifically, it didn't increase their increased receptive or expressive vocabulary. But this did rely on reporting from parents, so take the results with a pinch of salt.

However, 56% of parents said the baby video did "positively affect development" (p. 7, Rideout, 2007)

But I have no idea how they would know that?

How would parents know the DVD impacted positive and it wasn't the natural maturation of their child that was responsible for this positive development.

Consequently, parents might not be the best source of information about what babies are learning from video.

I can certainly agree with that point!

Another study of interest is Zimmerman, Christakis, & Meltzoff (2007)'s correlational study, remember we CANNOT establish cause and effect here.

The researchers interviewed 1,009 parents of 2 to 24-month-old infants by telephone to ask about babies' TV viewing habits, and parents completed a vocabulary checklist for the child using the MacArthur CDI.

The results showed for infants under 16 months each hour a day of TV viewing was associated with a 17 point drop in their vocabulary score.

However, this was not the case for toddlers.

I think this study is interesting because the results are possibly alarming, but this is correlational research, and we don't know exactly what's happening here.

But more research should be done into this area.

The final study we'll look at is DeLoache et al., (2010) who studied 72 infants aged 12 to 18 months and they were put into groups and they watched: a video with parent interaction, a Video with no interaction, no video with just a parent teaching the infant words or they were a control group, no teaching or video.

Afterwards, there were two tests: the initial visit and the final visit.

During the initial visit, the infants were tested on 13 words from the video and the words they didn't know became their personal 'target' list.

Afterwards, during the final visit, the infants were tested on their personal list and they were presented with objects in one order. Then the reverse order and the infant had to choose the object correctly both times for them to be credited with learning the word.

A bit harsh!

The results found the infants learnt very little from the baby videos and instead they learnt significantly more through parent-child interaction.

However, the parents were assessed as well.

Their assessment found a significant correlation between how much parents liked the video and how much the parents thought their children learned. With a Pearson coefficient of $r = .64$, and a p-value of $p < .01$)

Nonetheless, there was no correlation between how much parents thought their infant learnt and how well they did on the post-test.

In conclusion, parents may overestimate what their children are learning from videos.

Toddlers and Video:

So far, we've spoken a lot about how video affects infants, but what about toddlers?

To answer this question, the search task was created by Troseth, Saylor, & Archer (2006) who studied 24-month-old toddlers and these toddlers followed the instructions of people hiding behind a toy on the video.

So, the toddler thought the toy was talking to them.

The results showed the toddlers were 33% more likely to remember and use the information offered by the video.

Although, when the person in the video was interactive with the toddler and responding to them, this was done through CCTV. The toddlers were able to learn the information presented by the video.

Again, toddlers learn through interaction.

This is further supported by a word learning study by Roseberry et al (2013) where toddlers learnt a set of new verbs by someone teaching it to them live or being taught the verbs through a skype video call, or a pre-recorded video.

The results showed the toddler learned the words from the live interaction and the interactive video call, but not from the pre-recorded videos.

Meaning toddlers learn from interactive video and not pre-recorded ones.

Nevertheless, as much as I love these studies, it isn't always practical to use a video call.

So, can children ever learn educational content from pre-recorded videos?

They might be able to if the interaction is 'surrounding' the video. For instance, an interaction is happening between the parent and child while they both watch the video?

After all, this is similar to a child having their parents read a book to them, and this helps their reading.

<u>Content Matters:</u>

I've really enjoyed this chapter and I hope you have too.

All in all content matters because the videos have to be age-appropriate and interactive content, like Dora the Explorer, is better than fast-paced or adult-directed content.

CHAPTER 31: PRESCHOOLERS AND TELEVISION

On the whole, there is a lot of evidence that says children do learn from Sesame Street, as well as there's other research that shows watching programs as a pre-schooler relates to higher test scores.

Of course, it depends on the content, but more on that later.

This has been supported by Children's TV Workshop that carries out research every year since Sesame Street began.

What About Background TV?

In terms of pre-schoolers learning from TV, that's in the background and not what they're watching. Anderson & Hansen (2013) conducted two experimental studies with 3 years old pre-schoolers that spent on average 5.5 hours in the presence of background TV.

In the first study where the preschoolers played with a toy by themselves. The researchers found the amount of time spent playing with the toy was half as long when background TV was on than for kids who had no background TV on.

In addition, the researchers found the parents were less responsive to children's bids for attention and there was reduced language input & reduced "richness" of language.

In short, when there was background TV, the parents ignored their children more.

That's bad!

In the second study, which was a longitudinal study, a study that took place over time. The researchers found an increase in background TV on 6 months old predicted a preschooler decrease in cognitive and language development at 14 months old.

They found similar results at 1-year old since this negatively predicts executive functions at 4 years old.

Yet does screen media affect social skills?

Screen Media Exposure and Theory of Mind:

Mar, Tackett & Moore (2010) measured the correlation between media exposure, books, movies and TV, and children's theory of mind. They measured this by 'inferred experience.'

The researchers found inferred storybook and movie exposure correlated positively with theory of mind, but TV didn't.

Showing TV doesn't help children to develop intention reading, understanding and the other traits associated with theory of mind.

Promoting Preschoolers' Emotional Competence Through Prosocial TV and Mobile App Use

I must stress that TV and media isn't all bad for children because it can be used to promote prosocial behaviour. As seen in the Ding! Ding! Play Daniel's Trolley Game!

Therefore, in this game, children have fun driving the trolley and playing over 12 mini-games about feelings featuring Daniel and his friends.

For example, the game teaches children how to calm down by copying what Daniel does with a squeeze and a deep breath.

Another example is the game gets children to feel proud when they help Daniel clean up his toys and put away the silverware. And there are other examples, but you get the idea. The game aims to help children.

As a result, Rasmussen et al (2019) investigated

this game and they investigated the effects of different types of prosocial media on 121 preschoolers' emotion regulation and recognition.

In the groups, the children played with the Daniel app, played the app and watched the Daniel show or they played a control app, and they watched a control show.

The results found children who played the Daniel app as well as watched the show demonstrated the highest amounts of prosocial behaviour.

This has been further supported by Coyne et al (2018, p. 342) who said:

"[A]cross the 72 studies, 17,134 participants and 243 unique effect sizes were assessed, and findings suggested that prosocial media was positively associated with prosocial behaviour and empathic concern and negatively associated with aggression."

Another study of interest on the effects of media on children has to be Lillard & Peterson (2011) and they measured the impact of short-term exposure to fast-paced versus educational TV on children's executive function skills.

Their method was to get children to watch a fast-paced TV show for 9 minutes, an education clip for 9 minutes or get the children to partake in a self-paced drawing activity for 9 minutes.

Afterwards, they took part in a number of executive function tasks.

For example, The Tower of Hanoi, which tested problem-solving skills. As well as head, shoulder, knees and toes. Well, they did the American version called: head, toes, knees and shoulder. It took me ages to understand what this was. This tested self-regulation.

In addition, they did a test of delay of gratification. This tests the infant's inhibitory control. Then the infants were tested for their working memory by counting backwards from a number using a set digit span.

The results showed the content of the clip seemed to matter. Since the children who watched the fast-paced clip scored the worse. The children with the drawing activity did best at backwards digital and the tower activity.

Whereas children with the educational clip did best at Head, Shoulders, Knees and Toes and the delay of gratification task.

Does Screen Time Influence Mental Imagery?

In this area of research, there are two main hypothesises.

Firstly, there's the reduction hypothesis that

proposes viewing content on screens doesn't require active mental image construction.

As supported by "TV provides the viewer with ready-made visual images and thus does not provide viewers with practice in generating their own visual images." (Valkenburg & van der Voort, 1994)

Whereas the stimulation hypothesis proposes screen content primarily stimulates the visual and auditory, but it doesn't stimulate the motor, haptic or proprioceptive modalities.

CHAPTER 32: OVERALL: DO CHILDERN LEARN FROM SCREEN MEDIA?

On the whole, it depends on several factors. For example, the age of the child. Due to infants cannot learn from video, toddlers probably can't but preschoolers and older children might be able to.

Another factor it depends on is the type of screen media they are watching. For instance, is it educational, contingent or entertainment?

As a result, children are much more likely to learn from educational screen media compared to entertainment.

Finally, it depends on the outcome of interest that is studied. As shown throughout this section of the book, it depends on whether you're interested in language learning, social skills, imagination or comprehension on whether or not children can learn from screen media.

Summary:

Overall, educational screen media appears to be beneficial in a number of ways for preschoolers and older.

Also, children are spending more time in front of screens, as well as with new media, it will be important to study the impact on different types of development. For instance, the effects of artificial intelligence and voice speakers on development.

PART EIGHT: ADOLESCENCE

CHAPTER 33: ADOLESCENCE AND BIOLOGICAL TRANSITION

Personally, I think we can have a lot of fun with the topic of adolescence because it can be portrayed in a negative light. Since teenagers are typically moody, aggressive, etc and all that nonsense.

But as you'll see throughout this next section, teenagers are going through a series of changes and it can be difficult for them and their families.

The reason why I mentioned we can have fun in this topic is because I strongly believe this is one of the few areas of developmental psychology, we can apply directly to real life.

Therefore, I hope you will enjoy this section and hopefully get a few tips for yourself or your own family. Whether be it now or in the future.

Adolescence:

When we talk about adolescence, we're typically talking about a child or young person between the ages of 12 to 18 years old, and this is a time in a person's life where a lot of transitions are happening.

As a result, you have the biological and physical transition of puberty, you can the neurological transition since a lot of synaptic pruning occurs at this time, you have a cognitive transition as your cognitive development changes to the concrete formation operations as well as you experience a moral transition from the conventional to post-conventional level.

Finally, you have a social transition in terms of your education from primary to secondary school in the UK, or Elementary school to Middle School to the rest of the world.

Physical Transition:

The first transition we're going to look at is the physical or biological transition teenagers experience. Since this is the easiest to talk about and this is what everyone thinks of when they hear about adolescence.

The three major terms that are important to this transition is growth spurt, where people grow taller.

Another key term is menarche and I needed to

look it up and I was surprised. This is the term for a women's first menstrual cycle.

Then you have Spermarche. This is the first development of sperm in the testicles of a male.

The "Maturation Deviance Hypothesis"

Whilst we're discussing biological transitions, there's a hypothesis in developmental psychology that proposes deviances from the typical maturation process of teenagers leads to an increase in sociopsychological difficulties.

Thus, according to the hypothesis, if a person matures earlier or later than their peers this could result in problems for them.

As far as the research is concerned, this is only partially true because early maturing boys tend to be more positive self-concept, more popular, sportier and achieve higher at school.

Whereas early maturing girls tend to have more conflict with parents, more depression, less popular, show more risky behaviour and have more eating disorders.

If you're concerned for your teenager daughter, then there's a great research study later about how to possibly help.

Timing of Puberty:

Over the past 150 years, the age of menarche has decreased and whilst psychologists aren't sure why this has happened. One possible reason is because of improved nutrition so the bodies can develop faster.

Another possible reason is the effect of the family because oddly enough girls with a father tend to mature earlier in adolescence.

A final reason could be the social environment because the effects of early maturation are stronger in mixed-sex schools.

However, to counter this point, early maturation and rapid increases in hormones together are most risky for the negative effects of adolescence.

Adolescent Brain:

The final section in this biological chapter is the brain of a teenager goes through a lot of changes during adolescence.

From the myelination that occurs, this is the sheathing of nerve cells in fatty tissue increasing in white matter, to the new neural connections that are being formed that are followed by synaptic pruning. This eliminates excess neural connection and results in a decrease in grey matter. A lot occurs in the teenage brain.

And that's before we consider the hormones and the physiological changes in the brain where the brain structures are being modified.

As a result of this biological transition but by the person's experience and behaviour too.

CHAPTER 34: COGNITIVE TRANSITION

Not only do teenagers go through biological changes in adolescence but they go through a lot of psychological and cognitive changes as well.

Typically, these changes are referred to as a storm of emotion, stress and aggression with G. Stanley Hall (1904) saying "Youth are heated by nature as drunken men wine"

This is another way of summarising the changes in moods, risky behaviour and conflicts that a teenager can experience.

Personally, I think/ know teenagers get a bad rap because I remember being stopped constantly by security guards in certain shops because I was of that so-called age where I was of course going to shoplift.

If you ever met me in person and hopefully you can tell from the tone of this book I wouldn't shoplift. Yet I kept getting stopped.

Leading to us to Arnett (1999) when he asked the question does this really occur?

The research shows there is some disruption to a teenager's mood, there's an increase in conflict in early adolescence as well as there's an increase in risky behaviour. This peaks in late adolescence and in early adults.

Therefore, this is true to some extent because there is 'storm and stress' but this isn't inevitable.

Coleman's Model:

According to his model, most adolescents cope well with being a teenager and going through these changes.

Personally, I don't think this is a strange model because it makes sense because if a teenager has a supportive, understanding support system around them. Then their mental health should be fine.

(That's my clinical psychology book in one line for you!)

In addition, the model stresses that the adaptions peak at different points during adolescence, and the adaptions are spread over a number of years.

Consequently, the model proposes you need to deal with 1 issue then another and the problems, like the storm and stress, occur when you try to deal with more than one at a time.

Overall, you should be able to get through adolescence if you only focus on a few issues at a time.

Changes in Cognitive Ability:

Another major change teenager's experience is changes in their cognitive ability because new forms of thinking are available to them. Since Piaget (1972) proposes concrete formal operation thinking is now available to them. This helps them to understand abstract concepts and hypothetical deductive thoughts.

This helps teenagers to solve more complex problems as you can take more than one perspective into account.

However, the idea of formal operations has been criticised because these findings aren't always replicated and these aren't seen as universal.

Furthermore, adolescents continue to experience changes in thinking pass this stage as teenagers develop hypothetical reasoning. This continues into adolescence and adulthood.

Also, reasoning is the result of experience and training. As well as reasoning is domain-specific, not domain-general.

An interesting fact is cross-generational research shows teenagers are reaching the formal operational stage sooner. Since Fluller (1999) in 1967, 35% of 13 to 15 years old reached the formal operation stage compared to 55% in 1996.

Executive Control:

Due to changes in brain structure in relation to emotional regulation, response inhibition, planning and monitoring, adolescents can monitor and manage their own mental processes better.

This links to executive control because this requires knowledge and we all make decisions based on the relevance of information and the efficiency of our decision strategies.

All these improve during adolescents because of these brain changes.

Social Cognition:

Moving onto the changes teenagers experience in terms of social cognition, Elkind (1967) talks about adolescent egocentrism. This is where teenagers think about their own thoughts and they are aware other people have their own thoughts, but they fail to differentiate between them.

In other words, teenagers think their imaginary audience of others are as interested in them as you are in yourself.

Furthermore, teenagers experience an increase in their self -consciousness and they become more concerned about their appearance with an increased need for privacy and friends.

I think we can all relate to this point from our own adolescent experience.

However, like other changes, like conflict, that peak in early adolescence this does decrease. Since despite teenagers believing their own feelings are special and no one understands them. By the age of 16, they're more able to distinguish their own feelings.

Overall, egocentrism decrease in late adolescences.

<u>Moral and Political Reasoning:</u>

Personally, I love politics and I'm amazed by people's obsession with the old Conservative ways but this isn't a political book.

My point is during adolescence, teenagers are capable of more complex moral reasoning and this can be accelerated by parental intervention.

This results in the teenager experiencing a growth in political thinking. Meaning they can start to think about their own opinions and what they want for their future.

Moreover, this is further supported by there being a shift from concrete to abstract in their thinking and teenagers go through a decline in authoritarian solutions.

This allows teenagers to make their own decisions and opinions that are different from their family and friends.

In late adolescence, a broader ideology emerges. This helps them to understand the world and make political decisions.

CHAPTER 35: SOCIAL TIME AND FRIENDSHIP CHANGES IN ADOLESCENCE

The last set of changes to occur during adolescence are the social changes.

Personally, I think this is the most interesting area because I love social psychology, and in the next few chapters we'll going to explore a lot of social changes during this time.

What Is Social Time Spent On?

To ease us into the topic, the activities that make up social time for teenagers changes a lot. Since 40%-50% of their waking hours are spent on leisure activities for US and European adolescents.

Although, there are cross-cultural difference because Korean adolescents spent 20-30% of their time on leisure activities and Kenyan adolescents spent less than 10% of their time on leisure activities.

Interestingly, adolescents spend the greatest amount of time alone much of this alone time is media use, followed by peers then community/sports, then family.

Whilst some people might call this sad or unfortunate or 'how technology is destroying our lives' (I love that idea and laugh at it) We need to remember the cognitive and biological changes that are happening and the social changes that are occurring as well.

Digital Culture:

Digital culture is on the increase for better or for worse because in 2007, 55% of 13–17-year-olds had social media profiles whereas in 2015, 81% had social media profiles.

However, could social media be useful to explore self-clarity?

Since adolescents would be able to engage with other people, learn what they like and their own opinions.

Just a thought.

Changes in Friendships:

Apart of me wanted to put this chapter in Psychology of Relationships, but I wanted to keep everything together.

During adolescence, teenagers experience a lot of changes to their social groups because teenagers' main activity is talking to their friends, and it's important to note this is when they feel most happy.

Also, time with their peers increases from childhood until it exceeds time spent with any other social agent.

At the cost of time with their family decreasing over adolescence from 33% to 14% for children aged 10 to 18 years old.

Qualities of Friendships:

Furthermore, what's important in a friendship changes a lot because adolescents often refer to the importance of intimacy and loyalty in their friendships. (Yousin and Smoller, 1985)

Referring to the same study, Yousin and Smoller studied 1,049 adolescents from 12 to 17 years old, and they found characteristics by mutual intimacy were most important.

Due to 12 to 14 years olds rated intimacy and emotional support more important than 8- to 10-year-olds.

This is further supported by the fact 17 years olds report more intimacy between friends than 14 years old. (Rice & Mullen, 1995)

From my own personal experience, I can support the findings because I sort of defined an important friendship by how willing I am to share things with that person (psychological intimacy) and this started in my adolescence.

Another important change in friendships is friends want to be more equal and this links into equity theory in Social Psychology.

Moreover, similarity is important in friendships in adolescence because of several factors but in short, we like people who are more similar to us.

Yet adolescents don't seek friends to be identical to them.

In addition, Berndt & Houle (1985) found stability is another important change in adolescence because the researchers found Friendships increases in stability from childhood to early adolescence. As well as teenagers have an increased reluctance to make new friends.

I think we can all agree on the last point, can't we?

Gender Differences:

Throughout the chapter, I've explained the changes in friendships that occur but there are gender differences.

As a result, Rice & Mulkeen (1995) found girls rated themselves as more intimate with their best friends than boys. As well as girls spend more time with their best friends than boys.

Furthermore, Younus & Smoller (1985) found 45% of boys are the same as girls on intimacy and understanding in their friendships, and 30% of boys have non-intimate friendships.

Personally, I think that's a bit sad because I truly believe intimate friendships are important for mental health and well-being.

Since intimacy in friendships helps you to know you can turn to that person in your time of need, and you're not alone.

CHAPTER 36: ROMANTIC RELATIONSHIPS, CONFLICT WITH PARENTS AND NEED FOR AUTONOMY

Whenever people think of adolescence, they're bound to think about raging hormones and love struck teenagers and conflict with parents.

That's why we need to look at what's actually going on.

Romantic Relationships:

During adolescence, there's a shift towards other sex peers and teenagers tend to start thinking about relationships.

Whilst my university notes, talk about other sex peers and heterosexual relationships. It's fair to say there's a shift towards same-sex peers too if the adolescent is a homosexual.

All in all, teenagers start to become interested in dating and relationships.

Anyway, according to Brown's Model of Development of Romantic Relationship, which is based on the USA, there are a few stages that occur in this development.

Firstly, there's the Initiation phase. This is the onset of interest in someone the adolescent is romantically interested in.

Then the relationship starts.

Secondly, there the status phase where the teenager sees the relationship and the romance as a status enhancer.

Afterwards, you have the affection phase where the relationship develops so it is no longer as much as a status enhancer. As now the focus shifts to the relationship itself.

Then the final stage is the bonding phase, where in my experience and observations of other relationships, most relationships end. As a result, this is where people start to get concerned about commitment.

If you're interested in learning more about friendships and romantic relationships, please check out Psychology of Relationships.

Conflict With Parents:

This is probably the only 'true' stereotype of adolescence because conflict with parents does increase in early adolescence compared to childhood. As well as according to Shanahan et al., (2007) this conflict peaks at around the age of 13.

However, there are questions about whether there's a generation gap surrounding the topic of conflict with parents.

In other words, the source of the conflict with the parents being from another generation compared to the teenagers.

But the research shows this isn't the case and the parents and teenagers tend to report a good relationship overall.

As a result, they may conflict over apparently trivial issues, like dress, but they tend to agree on the more serious issues. Like: their education and their future, or the importance of planning for the future.

Therefore, this could represent a set of more fundamental concerns that the parents have?

There is no one answer to this question because parents and adolescents define conflicts differently. For example, the teenagers might argue the need for independence or personal autonomy but the parents might argue their problem is about social conventions.

Using a random example would be going your prom and your parents wanting to come but you didn't want them to.

You might argue you don't want them to come because you want to be more independent.

They might argue they have to go because it's the social norm.

I have no idea if it is or not, I don't remember my prom much, except it was boring and unneeded.

Subsequently, another answer to this question is teenagers are more likely to listen to their parents and their authority in some areas of their lives. Due to parents have lived experience, and they know how things work. Like: job interviews, relationship, etc.

<u>Is Conflict Always Bad?</u>

In short, conflicts can be beneficial in small amounts but high levels of conflict are never good. (Adams & Laursen, 2007)

Additionally, in my personal experience, I tend to find conflict can improve friendships sometimes. Since you get to talk it out and it can make you closer in certain situations.

Friends vs Parents:

This is certainly another area people tend to think about when someone mentions adolescence.

Although, this point or stereotype is often misunderstood because the common idea is teenagers will almost abandon their parents for their friends.

In truth, Rice & Mulkeen (1995) found intimacy with parents increased from 13 to 17 years olds and other research has shown the relationship transforms but it isn't severed.

A final common idea is the idea that a teenager will always be influenced more by their friends than their parents.

Again, in truth, Sebald (1986) found a teenager's friends and parents are two separate reference groups and both of these groups are part of their social network.

In other words, no one group has more influence over the adolescent.

Need for autonomy and Effects of Parenting Style:

Whenever we think of teenagers, we always think of them needing to be independent and they want to do whatever they want. This is sort of where the unruly teenager idea comes from.

However, the truth of the matter is adolescents don't want separation but they want individuation.

In other words, they want to be themselves and find out about the world, love and what they want.

This has research support because Steinberg & Silverberg (1986) studied adolescents from 10-14 years. The results found the adolescents had increased in their sense of self-control, and self-awareness.

In addition, adolescents go through de-idealisation of parents during this time. Since when we're children we tend to think our parents are the best and they know everything.

Another feature of adolescence is teenagers tend to have a decreased dependency on parents. This can be for a few reasons. For example, I remember my brother became more independent because he passed his driving test, and he spent a lot more time with his friends. So, he ate out a lot.

Leading us onto our next fact because these increases in independence are associated with other relationships. For instance, more time with friends and an adolescent's high autonomy is associated with high or higher celebrity interest.

However, the most important thing to remember during this talk about autonomy is teenagers can still have close parent-child relationships.

Different Types of Autonomy:

Overall, there are three types of autonomy an adolescent can have during adolescence.

Firstly, a teenager can go through emotional autonomy. This is where the adolescents, for lack of a better term, internalise their parents. So, they start to make their emotional decisions based on what their parents have taught them over the years.

Secondly, teenagers have behavioural autonomy. This is the overt manifestation of independent functioning.

In other words, this is the behaviour of the independent adolescent.

Lastly, an adolescent starts to develop their own system of values and morals. This is known as value autonomy.

Personally, I know during adolescence this is when I developed my beliefs about internationalism, my dislike for homophobia, racism and more.

Smetana's Social Domain Theory

This theory proposes adolescents and parents disagree with each other about autonomy in various domains.

Since parents can "violate" an adolescent's sense of autonomy and this can lead to conflict.

To overcome this conflict, it is important for both adolescents and parents to clarify domain boundaries.

Effect of Parenting Style:

You can probably guess that the parenting style of a person is very important because according to research the optimal style is authoritative. As well as the parenting being a warm, loving home structure and autonomy support.

In other words, the best parenting style for adolescents is a warm loving home environment with a supportive family.

According to Lamborn et al (1991), this is associated with healthy adolescent development in terms of their psychosocial competence, as well as their educational achievement.

Additionally, parents need to balance their teenagers' autonomy (independence) with the need of protecting them by restricting their freedom.

This might seem harsh but this can have developmental benefits. Since it can facilitate an adolescent's intellectual development through reasoning and negotiation with their parents.

Interestingly, during adolescence, teenagers identify more with their parents. This could be down to a few reasons. For example, towards the end of adolescence, teenagers tend to get jobs and they have more responsibility. Allowing them to relate more to their parents.

However, the directionality of this effect isn't understood. Because are the teenagers identifying more with their parents because of jobs and responsibilities?

Or are the parents identifying more with their teenagers because they are reminded about their own teenage struggles?

CHAPTER 37: PERSONALITY, IDENTITY AND SELF DEVELOPMENT

In the future, I will be doing a personality book but until then this small section on the personality of adolescents will have to do.

Therefore, Erikson (1968) proposed the Stage model of personality development where each stage has a psychological task.

As a result of during adolescence, teenagers can experience many personality changes. For example, identity vs identity diffusion. Also known as confusion.

This occurs because adolescence is a time in a person's life of asking 'Who am I?' and a period of searching during which identity not achieved – psychological moratorium.

In other words, this is where teenagers look for who they are and how they want to identify themselves.

During this time, people can experiment with different roles.

This can range from Sexuality to their chosen job to other identities.

I remember a friend of a friend decided to experiment with their Sexuality to see if they were a lesbian or not. After some experimenting with their identity, they decided that they weren't.

Personally, my identity changed a lot during this time because I became interested in psychology and started to write fiction books.

Of course, most people have more normal personalities.

If the identity of the adolescent isn't resolved this can lead to the teenager developing a self-perceived foreclosure or negative identity.

According to Marcia (1980), this is a formal measure of an adolescent identity status and there are a range of terms that can be used to describe identity.

For instance, identity diffusion is when the person experiences an avoidance of commitment.

Whereas identity foreclosure is when someone is committed to beliefs but is not self-determined.

In addition, if a person suffers identity Moratorium (great work!) then they're experiencing a state of crisis. This is where the adolescent is exploring possibilities.

Subsequently, you have identity achievement. This when an adolescent experiences an identity crisis but resolves it and doesn't avoid commitment.

Does Identity Status Matter?

I understand why people might think identity status doesn't matter but it is linked to other aspects of an adolescent's development. Such as their romantic attachments, anxiety and self-esteem. Without identity status, these other aspects could be inhibited and definitely impacted for better or for worse.

Furthermore, the style or type of identity that adolescents decide to have is a process rather than an outcome.

Building upon this further, there are three board types or styles of identity an adolescent can have. These are: Informational, normative or diffuse-avoidant.

Interestingly, each of these styles has their own unique ways of dealing with stress and anxiety. For example, people with informational style show defence mechanisms that control anxiety and threats by using cognitive manoeuvres.

Whereas people with normative identity styles, protect themselves against threats and information by using denial and distortion tricks.

Finally, people with the diffuse-avoidant style tend to have lower self-esteem, optimism and efficacy as well as higher levels of delinquent attitudes and hopelessness (Phillips & Pittman, 2007)

Self-Concept In Adolescence

So, the developments from childhood continue with the adolescents differentiating themselves from other people (Optimal distinctiveness), organising the parts of themselves into one whole self and integrating the different parts of themselves. Allowing these parts to fit together.

By mid-adolescence, the teenagers find some of their identities contradict one another and they find these contradictions confusing.

Possibly, leading to the problems we have discussed previously.

By late adolescence, the concept of the self becomes more integrated and there is a decline in the importance of social reference groups. Since the teenager knows who they are. As well as there is an emphasis on internalised thoughts, beliefs and motives.

In short, the adolescent knows who they are now and they can be more independent.

Do Adolescents Undergo Identity Crisis?

After reading all this, I cannot blame you in the slightest about thinking teenagers undergo an identity crisis. But whilst there are attempts to define the self and their identity. There is not necessarily a "crisis".

Therefore, some researchers have proposed that the notion of the identity crisis could be culturally biased.

For instance, identity foreclosure may be more optimal than achievement in some societies.

Moreover, whilst some researchers think the whole identity development of adolescence could be prolonged by education. It is important to note identity statuses do not always represent the developmental sequence.

As a result, identity isn't a single event or a short-term process as well as changes in identity can be gradual rather than discontinuous.

Summary:

Overall, during adolescence, the time spent with friends increases whilst the time spent with family decreases.

With the friendships becoming more intimate, along with the new interest in romantic relationships.

In addition, the need for autonomy leads to changes in the parent-adolescent relationship which may result in conflict, but this can be avoided.

Finally, establishing a sense of identity is one of the primary psychological tasks of adolescence, but can be achieved without experiencing an identity crisis.

The most important thing to remember is that successful adolescence results in independent adult individual.

PART NINE: ATYPICAL DEVELOPMENT

CHAPTER 38: ATYPICAL DEVELOPMENT

The vast majority of this book focuses on how children develop in a 'normal' situation and whilst I hate the term normal. It is applicable in this chapter. Since sometimes children develop in an atypical way.

But as a person who falls under this category, I wanted to say this doesn't make a child strange or disabled. It just makes them different.

To kick off this chapter, we need to talk about the idea of domain-general skills and behaviours since this might be wrong.

<u>Evaluating Domain General Accounts:</u>

Casting our minds back to the idea of domain-general and specific skills, the idea of skills and behaviours being domain specific is interesting because it provides us a powerful and parsimonious explanation for how a particular skill or behaviour develops.

However, it doesn't explain the development of key skills or behaviours in people with uneven profiles. In other words, people who have typically developed.

That's why I thought I would this chapter that way because developmental conditions can involve very specific impairments depending on the condition.

Therefore, how is this possible if development in thinking is domain-general?

This Brings Us To Cognitive Neuropsychology

The Cognitive Neuropsychological Perspective

Cognitive Neuropsychology:

If we want to understand how conditions can impact development, we need to understand how they can affect our mental processes.

Consequently, if cognitive processes are dissociated, it implies that they must operate at least partially independently. This is another way of saying they must be Domain-specific. (Shallice, 1988)

For example, in Broca's aphasia. A person can comprehend but struggle to produce speech.

In Wernicke's aphasia, people can produce fluent

speech but it's off topic and random. This suggests they have little comprehension of speech.

Theories To How General Learning Processes Mechanisms Account For Double Associations:

Modularity:

Yes, I know the subtitles above were horrible and long- sorry.

According to Carruthers (2006), our cognition is made up of domains specific, innately specific modules and our cognitive skills come from domain specificity of function.

In other words, we are born with modules in our brains that control certain cognitive skills exclusively. This is built on the original concept of modularity by Fodor (1983)

Core Knowledge Theory:

According to Spelke & Kinzler (2007), humans are endowed with five domains- specific or modular core knowledge systems that operate from early infancy. These are where new flexible skills and knowledge are built upon.

In addition, humans have a core understanding of numbers, actions, objects, space and social partners.

You can think of this as we have an innate

understanding of how actions, objects and numbers work. But we understand the importance of social partners as well.

Developmental Cognitive Neuropsychology:

This is a subarea of cognitive psychology that aims to apply to the logic of cognitive neuropsychology to children. (Temple, 1997; Leslie, 1992; Baron-Cohen, 1998)

This field of study assumes that our modules are innate and brain is modular in nature from the start.

They think this is due to the associated evolutionary advantages because damage to one modular wouldn't lead to the failure of the whole system.

Leading us into developmental disorders, but if you've read my other books you know I prefer the term conditions and my reasons behind that, that involve selective cognitive impairments are examples of intact and impaired modules.

Like, autism and Williams Syndrome.

CHAPTER 39: WILLIAMS SYNDROME

The first condition, we'll look at is Williams Syndrome and this is an interesting condition that sounds okay at first but it can be an awful condition to have.

This was first identified by cardiologist William and colleagues in 1961 with it having a prevalence rate ranging from 1 in 20,000 (Morris et al, 1988) to 1 in 7,500 (Stromne et al, 2002)

People who have this condition have certain facial characteristics. Including fully prominent lips, a wide mouth, small and widely spaced teeth, a short nose, a star-like iris pattern as well as prominent ear lobes

In addition, Williams syndrome is caused by the deletion of around 26 genes from the chromosome 7a11.23 (Peoples et al, 2000)

If you like silver linings, one positive is this. It

allows identification of the condition at birth so we can study development as a result.

Personality Profile:

I always think personality is interesting. Especially, when different conditions affect it. For example, in Williams Syndrome, sufferers tend to have a personality of hyper sociability, a tendency to fixate on faces and smile frequently, social disinhibition where they show a high degree of empathy and concern for others, they appear to exude happiness, as well as they show hyperactivity.

Furthermore, children with this condition are rated as more empathetic, sensitive and gregarious then typically developed children or children with other developmental disorders. (Brock et al, 2008)

Personally, I think if you only knew about these personality traits then you might think this condition was positive and they were minimal drawbacks.

That's until we start to look at the cognitive impacts of the condition.

Cognitive Profile:

Interestingly and unfortunately, Williams syndrome is characterised by an uneven cognitive profile.

It's uneven because there is a delay in cognitive development. Resulting in a low IQ of around 55. (Mortens et al, 2008)

Although, there are particular toughs and peaks too. This is a weird way of saying strengths and Weaknesses.

Generally, people with this condition have numerical and visual-spatial skills that are significantly impaired.

However, some people claim language and social cognition are intact. Hence, the uneven profile.

Does WS Provide Evidence For Modularity?

Whilst, there is barely any official research on the topic of Williams syndrome and modularity. There is anecdotal evidence of a dissociation between visuospatial and language skills.

Since in terms of behaviour, the child's language and visuo-spatial ability appear to be dissociated in people with Williams syndrome. Due to Rossen et al. (1995): says *"Williams syndrome presents a remarkable juxtaposition of impaired and intact mental capacities: linguistic functioning is preserved in WS while problem-solving ability and visuospatial cognition are impaired."*

Nonetheless, when you compare people with Williams syndrome and other developmental conditions with specific language impairment. This may provide evidence of a double dissociation.

Specific Language Impairments:

Whilst, this might seem as if we're going off track and away from Williams Syndrome, I promise you we will return to that condition in a moment.

Meanwhile, specific language impairments are when a child's language abilities are significantly below age expectations in one or more language domains.

In terms of statistics, you probably have a language impairment if your language score is equal to or greater than 1.25 *SD* below the mean, as well as people with a specific language impairment tend to have a normal non-verbal performance with an IQ equal to or greater than 85 with no apparent sensory or neurological dysfunction.

The Discrepancy Between Language And Intelligence:

There has been a lot of research over the years to show just because you have a high IQ, it doesn't mean you have good language skills. Since this is what a 14 year old boy said with a specific language impairment with a very high IQ of 118 points.

"Yesterday jump in a river...uhm...get new shoe... shoe wet. Mummy cross. Her looking for brother. Her go everywhere... uhm... not find him. Hide behind tree...uhm... very naughty." (Karmiloff & Karmiloff-Smith, 2001, p.190)

Therefore, this shows high general intelligence doesn't mean you always have good language skills.

Furthermore, this is shown by another 14 year

old boy with Williams Syndrome with a very low IQ score of only 59 points.

"Yesterday your naughty brother jumped into a river. It was shallow. He did it on purpose. Now that's a stupid thing to do, isn't it! He got his new shoes all wet and slimy. This made his mum exasperated. He knew he was in trouble, so he hid behind a tree so she wouldn't find him. Oh boy, he'll probably get a whale of a telling off. My mother gets furious if I dare go against her wishes. Was he grounded?" (Karmiloff & Karmiloff-Smith, 2001, p.199)

Overall, this suggests there is a double dissociation between language and non-verbal intelligence as Pinker (1999) explains *"overall, the genetic* **double dissociation** *is striking .... The genes of one group of children [with SLI] impair their grammar while sparing their intelligence; the genes of another group impair their intelligence while sparing their grammar"* (p. 293)

Is Visuo-Spatial Processing Impaired In WS?

According to Stinton et al. (2008) who explored the mental rotation ability in 15 adults with Williams syndrome and 15 typically developed children. The researchers found the two groups matched in non-verbal intelligence using Raven's Coloured Progressive Matrices. This is a test of nonverbal reasoning.

Then the mental rotation task involved presenting pairs of shapes and asking whether they were the same or different. They found participants with Williams Syndrome were significantly poorer than the typically developed participants.

Thus, mental rotation skill is poorer in Williams Syndrome than expected on the basis of overall non-verbal intelligence as well as age.

Is Visuo-Spatial Cognition Intact In SLI?

To answer this question, Guarnera et al. (2013) studied 7-year-olds with a specific language impairment (SLI), and age- and gender-matched typical children. The researchers showed the children pictures of hands rotated 0-270 degrees and asked them is it a left or right hand?

The researchers found there were no group differences in accuracy or speed on this or another test of mental rotation.

Consequently, visuo-spatial cognition is intact.

CHAPTER 40: AUTISM SPECTRUM CONDITIONS

Autism is a condition that is close to my heart and I love it.

Despite all the misconceptions, there are about Autism. I wouldn't give it up for the world.

Of course, it can be difficult, but I think there are a lot of advantages too.

Plus, I know I've said this before but I will certainly not use the term Disorder to describe Autism, and neither would my friends.

Anyway, this CONDITION has several impairments as described by the Diagnostic and Statistical Manual Version 5.

Please see Abnormal Psychology for more information.

For instance, people with autism have social communication difficulties. Meaning communicating with others and social skills can be difficult.

Personally, I tend to be described as blunt and this has gotten better with age, but I hate small talk, and I would rather tell a person how it is. But over time I have learnt how to answer questions better.

Some other difficulties are non-verbal communication, developing and understanding relationships and overlaps with restricted, repetitive behavioural and interests.

On a personal note, I find making friends so difficult. The social groups, what you're meant to say and all that 'easy' social stuff I do not understand.

This probably explains why my best friends over the years all have been autistic or have had autistic relatives.

I don't know why exactly but it is so much easier talking to another autistic person than a 'normal' person.

The final two difficulties or impairments for people with autism are highly restricted fixated interest, as well as a strong insistence on sameness or inflexible adherence to routine.

This has definitely improved over time, but I still hate change and I absolutely hate with a passion something that changes my routine.

Of course, I don't mention it but inside I do get annoyed.

Also, on the fixated interests note, my life is basically all about psychology but most of all I love to learn everything about writing, publishing and the author life.

Considering I never talk about autism in public (yes, this book counts as public) I'm liking it.

Spectrum:

Autism is considered a spectrum because the severity of its features varies across individuals and the severity varies over time.

For instance, I'm not very severe and you would look at me and say I'm normal. But if I told you I was autistic then certain things would make sense to you.

Additionally, in the DSM-5 the level of language difficulties and intelligence are specified as well. This replaces the old distinction between autistic and Asperger's conditions.

My language was awful growing up. I needed two years of speech therapy for starters!

Social Modules:

In the last chapter, we spoke about Williams syndrome and these social modules are hyper-social and heightened empathy.

Whereas autism leaves people apparently socially impaired and with diminished empathy (a bit harsh!)

Also, Bellugi et al. (1999, p.200) mentions:

Individuals with Williams syndrome *"exhibit a striking contrast to the social and language profiles of individuals with other disorders such as autism".*

Although, these conditions do provide some evidence for "social" because these features of the conditions show that language isn't the only ability that researchers have argued is intact in Williams syndrome.

Since in Williams Syndrome Face-processing & "theory of mind" are seen as strengths and some researchers take this as evidence of the modularity of social-cognitive functions (see Karmiloff-Smith et al., 1995)

Nonetheless, this raises the question of is there a double dissociation in autism with facial processing and Theory of Mind impaired? And by extension Social Cognition?

Well, many studies use standardised tasks. Like the Benton Faces task or different versions of it. This is where the participant is shown an image of a target face.

Next, they're shown a selection of 6 faces and asked to pick the one that matches the target.

These faces can be shown at different orientations and/or in different lighting conditions as well.

One such study is Croydon et al. (2014) that used a variant of the Benton faces task using 7- to 12-year-olds with autism and age-matched typically developed children.

The researchers found there was a significant recognition impairment for the children with autism. As well as the severity of the autism correlated with face recognition performance.

Meaning the more severe the autism in the child, the worse the facial recognition.

Whereas people with Williams Syndrome tend to have normal performance. That is the performance that is showed by typically developed children. (Farran & Jarrold, 2003; Tager-Flusberg, Plesa-Skwerer, Faja, & Joseph, 2003; Karmiloff-Smith et al., 2004)

Consequently, the evidence that face recognition is age-appropriate contrasts with the fact that face processing in autism is significantly poorer than people with Williams Syndrome. (Riby et al., 2008)

Ultimately, this provides us evidence for the social module with which we use to innately process faces is intact in Williams Syndrome but impaired in Autistic people. (Bellugi et al., 1994; Boucher et al., 1992)

However, you cannot think I'm done just yet. Because is it possible a poor performance could still result in high competency?

As a result, only cognitive functions are said to exist in modules or be domain-specific, and the measures for these functions never purely measure the strategy.

Therefore, it is possible that superficially face processing is intact, but the task performance relies on an alternative, compensatory or atypical strategy to get the job done. And it is these atypical strategies that the measure measures and that is the poor performance. (Deruelle et al. (1999); Karmiloff-Smith, Brown, Grice, Paterson, 2003)

To conclude this chapter, is representation of cognition impaired in autism?

So, we know theory of Mind is the ability to represent the mental states of other people and there is a large and reliable deficit on classic false-belief tasks showed by autistic people. Which can be termed horribly as saying autistic people show the results for these tasks as below the expected standard for their mental age. (Yirmiya et al., 1998, Psychological Bulletin, 124, 283-307)

Therefore, the research shows that autistic people do lack Theory of Mind and I know I've spoken about this in another book but I think there's a caveat to this research.

Nonetheless, I know Theory of Mind is difficult because nine times out of ten I have no idea why people are annoyed. I try to think about this sometimes but other times it's too difficult to try and work out why they're annoyed or upset.

CHAPTER 41: DEVELOPMENT OF METACOGNITION: A GUIDE TO METACOGNITION, METAMEMORY, MORE AND ITS IMPORTANCE

As always, there are certain things you never hear about until you do certain topics in psychology. This is one of them. Never before had I heard of metacognition.

Anyway, metacognition is our ability to represent our own states.

In essence, it is thinking about thinking and becoming aware you are having your own thoughts.

This is important when you think about Theory of Mind, this is our awareness of the mental state of others, and you cannot have ToM without metacognition.

So, it's pretty important.

Yet this is another example of several complex cognitive processes because Schneider (2008) decided to create the taxonomy of metacognition components.

According to this taxonomy, metacognition involves declarative skills as well as procedural skills, like monitoring and controlling our thinking and emotions.

Again, to us adults it sounds simple but it takes a while for us to be able to develop these skills.

Leading us to Nelson's and Narens' (1990) model of procedural metacognition. This refers to procedural skills rather than declarative knowledge. With these cognitive processes split into two interrelated levels. The object-level and meta-level.

These levels allow us to think about thinking about thinking at the same time.

Like in a presentation, a presenter is thinking about the current slide, but is starting to think about the next slide, realises thoughts are wordiness.

Tests Of Online Meta-Monitoring

Tests of memory monitoring involves the participants making online judgements about their states of knowledge, memory and learning.

They are lots of tests for meta-monitoring. Like: measuring meta-monitoring accuracy. This is determined by comparing objective knowledge, actual performance, with a person's judgments about the degree of one's knowledge.

Then you measure the correlation between the judgements of performance and actual performance. The higher the accuracy, the better your metacognitive monitoring ability.

Developmental Studies Of Judgments Of Learning

When it comes to understanding how we judge learning, there are several researchers who have looked at this area.

For instance, Lipowski et al (2013) explored judgements of learning in preschoolers, children aged between 4 and 5, and people in the third grade. So, children between the ages of 8 and 9 years old.

Then the children learnt the names of 12 or 18 stuffed animals.

After a 2 minute delay, the children were asked to make judgements of learning, and after a 30-second delay, they were given a final recall test.

The study found there were significant age-related improvements in the accuracy of the judgements of learning.

This was explained because the poorer performance by the preschoolers was due to their overconfidence.

Developmental Studies Of Feeling Of Knowing

Another subarea of metacognition is all about how we believe we're able to retrieve specific information.

One study that explored this was Cultice et al. (1983) that explored feelings of knowledge in 4- and 5-year-olds. In their study, there were 3 phases.

Firstly, you had the naming phase where children were shown pictures of people of varying familiarity. Like, people, they knew well and people that were unknown to them. Then the children were asked to name them. This would allow the children to develop a cue for when they had to recall them later on.

Afterwards, you had the Feelings of Knowledge phase where the children were shown the pictures of the people they hadn't been able to name in the last phase for a second time, and the researchers asked them:

- Whether they had or hadn't seen the person before.
- Whether they (the child) thought they could pick out their name if the researchers gave them some options.

Finally, there was the recognition phase. This is where the children were presented with a target picture along with a few age and sex-matched distraction pictures. Then the children were asked to pick out the one called a name from earlier.

The results showed that both the groups performed better than chance. This is an extremely weird way to say the researchers reached the p-value. Or there was a less than 5% chance that the results were down to luck.

Also, there wasn't any bias towards overconfidence or under-confidence in either of the group, as well as there were no age differences, suggesting feelings of knowing are monitored from age 4.

In other words, children are able to retrieve specific pieces of information.

What Is Metamemory Control?

Our final type of metacognition is metamemory and this is our ability to recognise and think about our own memory processing.

So, meta-level exerts more top down control over object-level metacognition and if we speak more broadly, control refers to translating the output of our thinking and monitoring into an adaptive or useful behavioural response. This is related to our executive functioning.

Consequently, it's vital to look at control because the processes of control and monitoring are interlinked. Thus you can monitor your thoughts without controlling them, but you cannot control your thoughts if you haven't' monitored them or at least thought about them first.

Overall, control refers to how we can change our behaviour based on our learning and on our thinking or opinion of the situation.

We can study this metamemory control by strategically getting people to answer specific questions, using "opting out" of tough trials, seeking help on tough trials but this most often measured during Judgement of control or uncertainty monitoring tasks.

Strategic Selection Of Answers

This method is done by testing the child's performance on object-level task. For example, answering questions or selecting the correct item or giving answers for items that they studied before they were taken away.

After the child answered and they often made a judgement of confidence, the participants were asked whether the answer should be kept or discarded. The key measures in this test was if the kept answers were any more likely to be correct than incorrect, and is object-level performance improved by the exclusion of items?

Uncertainty And Metamemory Control

To test this, Hembacher and Ghetti (2014) used a judgment of confidence task with 3 to 5-year-olds infants to assess metamemory monitoring and control.

In the study phase of the study, the children were presented with 30 items in an order and some were presented twice. Then the children were given a recognition memory test followed by a confidence of judgement test. This was to look at their monitoring/control skills.

The results showed a range of answers because there were no differences across the ages for the recognition memory test.

For the confidence judgement, the 3-year-old children showed no evidence of memory monitoring, also known as metamemory. Yet the 4 and 5-year-olds showed clear evidence of memory monitoring.

Finally, the results for the test that looked at meta-cognitive control found the kept items were more likely to be correct than incorrect and excluded items more likely incorrect than correct

But this was only found among 4- and 5- year-olds.

Metacognition and ASD

When it comes to metacognition and people with Autism Spectrum Conditions, everyone agrees that people with these conditions have difficulty recognizing others' mental states. I can relate!

In addition, it is accepted that autistic people's failure on theory of mind tasks reflect a lack of competence, not just poor performance.

Personally, I think that's horribly worded but this fact is trying to say autistic people lack the ability to do intention reading and other skills a part of the Theory of Mind.

However, some researchers would argue that self-awareness of mental states is intact in autistic people (Goldman, 2006; Nichols & Stich, 2003)

Personally, I have found this to be the case in certain situations when I have to think and focus on myself, but other times, this is beyond me. For example, when I'm, being blunt and I'm just talking.

Therefore, if this is the case that autistic people have self-awareness but poor Theory of Mind, it provides evidence that metacognition is separate and, some argue prior, to mindreading and other areas of the Theory of Mind.

Unexpected Contents Task – Smarties Task

In all honesty, this section is very similar to when we looked at the Sally-Anne task in the theory of mind section of the book since this is a classic Theory of Mind measure. The focus of this measure is the other-person question of "What will *someone else* think is inside before they look?" versus the self-test question of "What did *you* think was inside before you looked"

Overall, this measures your own false belief and this has been assessed using the smarties task.

In this task, someone comes in with a tube of smarties and says "what is in this tube?" then the Child says Smarties. This is perfectly logical then because I'm a bit mean I think it's funny when the researcher opens the tube and shows that there were pencils inside. And it's the end of the world for that child!

Yes, I'm horrible for smiling as I wrote that line!

Afterwards, someone else comes in and the researcher asks the child "what does Billy think is in the tube?" now the correct answer is pencils and the incorrect answer is Smarties.

Personally, I don't understand why because I think Billy must think the same as the child here. But I guess that's just my ASD showing up.

Anyway, this is the Theory of Mind element of the test and children with autism tend to not do very well here.

Then there's a final question. Which is what did you think was inside the box before you looked? And of course, the correct answer is Smarties.

I got that one right!

And this is a measure of your own false belief. So, can you access your own belief from a previous moment?

Understanding Own False Belief In ASD

Two very early studies on the topic found amazing results on the smarties test. For instance, Perner et al. (1989) found that only 17% of autistic people passed the Other-person test question but 100% passed the Self test question.

This is further supported by Leslie & Thaiss (1992) that found 27% passed the Other-person test question whereas 67% passed the Self test question.

The results show that autistic people understand their own mind before understanding the minds of others. Which I completely agree with. Half of the time I don't bother trying to understand other people because it's too difficult for me.

In terms of the wider field of metacognition, it suggests that metacognition relies on a separate process or mechanism to mind reading.

Practical Implications of Metacognition

All throughout this very long chapter, I've spoken about metacognition and its different subareas. But why does it matter?

I ask this because we can all probably agree that some areas of psychology are... useless in everyday life. As well as there is no clear benefit to this knowledge at first.

Me and my personality coursework partner were talking about this issue this morning as I write this. Since for our coursework, we want to make sure it would be considered a meaningful contribution to psychology if it was real.

Anyway, metacognition is not pointless, at first it might seem it, but there are several key uses for knowledge about metacognition.

For instance, in education, metacognition is key to children being able to be effective at self-guided learning.

In addition, metacognition allows us to inform eyewitness testimony better because if you've read Forensic Psychology then you know how bad eyewitnesses can be in certain contexts. But metacognition is important because our ability to be able to tell the "whole truth and nothing but the truth" relies on accurate metacognition.

Metacognition And Academic Success

Building upon this further, metacognition is very important to academic performance because it allows children to have accurate monitoring of their learning and memory is important because it allows through the process of control: to decide what topics we want to study, it allows us to allocate study time and stop studying a particular topic. As well as allows us to use an appropriate strategy and decide what exam question or questions to answer.

Overall, I think it's fair to say metacognition is pretty vital when it comes to education and both under- and overconfidence can be detrimental to a child's success.

Metacognition and Exam Success in Psychology Students

One researcher decided to investigate how metacognition impacts the exam success of psychology students and his researchers only reinforce what the literature states.

Therefore, Hacker et al. (2000) asked undergraduate psychology students to predict the percentage of questions they would answer correctly before and after each of their three exams.

The results show there was a positive relationship between the accuracy of the student's predictions, monitoring metacognition, and their exams mark, object-level.

Furthermore, the students who performed the worst on the exam where the students who have the most overconfident predictions.

So, don't be overconfident!

The Dunning-Kruger Effect: Unskilled and Unaware Of It

This is an interesting effect, I wanted to add into the book.

"This lack of awareness arises because poor performers are doubly cursed: Their lack of skill deprives them not only of the ability to produce the correct responses, but also of the expertise necessary to surmise that they are not producing them." (Dunning et al., 2003, p.83).

I say this effect is interesting because it shows both object-level and meta-level problems that can happen to people. For example, the double burden of ignorance is object-level and the meta-ignorance is operating at the meta-level.

Is Metacognition Just About Intelligence?

To complete this long chapter on metacognition, I need to mention that whilst metacognitive skills are related to IQ. This is not a perfect relationship as well as IQ and metacognitive skills make independent contributions to academic performance (Veenman et al., 2004)

For example, Veenman et al. (2005) found that metacognitive strategy use was significantly correlated with mathematic ability even after controlling for IQ. This study suggests that even if you take out IQ, metacognition makes its own contribution to mathematic ability.

Consequently, both intelligence and metacognition are important factors in predicting a child's academic success.

BIBLIOGRAPHY

Lee Parker (author), Darren Seath (author) Alexey Popov (author), *Oxford IB Diploma Programme: Psychology Course Companion,* 2nd edition, OUP Oxford, 2017

Alexey Popov, *IB Psychology Study Guide: Oxford IB Diploma Programme,* 2nd edition, OUP Oxford, 2018

Gillibrand, R., Lam, V. & O'Donnell, V.L. (2016). Developmental psychology (2nd ed.). London: Prentice Hall.

Adams & Laursen (2007) The correlates of conflict: Disagreement is not necessarily detrimental. *Journal of Family Psychology,* 21, 445-458

Baumrind (1989) Rearing competent children. In W.Damon (Ed.) *Child development today and tomorrow* (pp.349-378). San Francisco: Jossey-Bass.

Berndt, Hawkins, & Hoyle (1986) Changes in

friendships during a school year. Effects on children and adolescents' impressions of friendship and sharing with friends. *Child Development, 57,* 1284-1297

Berndt & Hoyle (1985) Stability and change in childhood and adolescent friendships. *Developmental Psychology,* 21, 1007-1015.

Elkind, D. (1967) Egocentrism in adolescence. *Child Development,* 38, 1025-1034

Flieller, A. (1999) Comparison of the development of formal thought in adolescent cohorst aged 10 to 15 years (1967-1996 and 1972-1993). *Development Psychology,* 35, 1048-1058

Giles & Maltby (2004) The role of media figures in adolescent development: relations between autonomy, attachment and interest in celebrities. *Personality and Individual Differences,* 36, 813-822

Graber, J., Brooks-Gunn, J., & Warren, M. (2006) Pubertal effects on adjustment in girls: Moving from demonstrating effects to identifying pathways. *Journal of Youth and Adolescence,* 35, 413-423

Inhelder & Piaget (1958) *The growth of logical thinking from childhood to adolescence.* New York: Basic Books

Kroger, J. (2004) *Identity in adolescence.* Routledge: London

Macintosh & Dissanayake (2004). "The similarities and differences between autistic disorder and Asperger's disorder: A review of empirical evidence". Journal of Child Psychology and Psychiatry, 45, 421-434.

Lamborn, Mounts, Steinburg, & Dornbusch (1991) Patterns of competence and adjustment among adolescents from authoritative, authoritarian, indulgent and neglectful families. *Child Development,* 62, 1049-1065

Phillips, & Pittman (2007) Adolescent psychological well-being by identity style. *Journal of Adolescence, 30,* 1021-1034

Rice & Mulkeen (1995) Relationships with parents and peers: A longitudinal study. *Journal of Adolescent Research* , 10, 338-357

Piaget (1972). *Judgement and reasoning in the child.* Towota, NJ: Littlefield Adams

Sebald (1986) Shifting orientation towards parents and peers: A curvilinear trend over recent decades. *Journal of Marriage and the Family*, 48, 5-13.

Shanahan, McHale, Osgood, & Crouter (2007) Conflict frequency with mothers and fathers from middle childhood to late adolescence: Within- and between-families comparisons. *Developmental Psychology,* 43, 539-550

Smetana (2011) *Adolescents, families and social development.* Chichester, UK: Wiley-Blackwell

Steinberg & Silverberg (1986) The vicissitudes of autonomy in early adolescence. *Child Development, 57,* 841-851.

Youniss & Smollar (1985) *Adolescent relations with mothers, fathers and friends.* Chicago: University of Chicago Press

Hamann, K., Warneken, F., Greenberg, J. R., & Tomasello, M. (2011). Collaboration encourages equal sharing in children but not in chimpanzees.

Hepach, Vaish, Tomasello (2012). Young children are intrinsically motivated to see others helped.

Liszkowski, Carpenter, Striano, & Tomasello (2006). 12-and 18-month- olds point to provide information for others.

Schmidt & Sommerville (2011). Fairness expectations and altruistic sharing in 15-month-old human infants.

Svetlova, Nichols, & Brownell (2010). Toddlers' prosocial behavior: From instrumental to empathic to altruistic helping.

Warneken & Tomasello (2006). Altruistic helping

in human infants and young chimpanzees.

Warneken & Tomasello (2008). Extrinsic Rewards Undermine Altruistic Tendencies in 20-Month-Olds.

Warneken & Tomasello (2013). Parental presence and encouragement do not influence helping in young children.

Grusec et al. Prosocial and helping behavior. In: Smith & Hart (Eds.) Blackwell handbook of childhood social development. Malden, MA: Blackwell Publishing; 2002.

https://www.subscribepage.com/psychology boxset

Thank you for reading.

I hoped you enjoyed it.

If you want a FREE book and keep up to date about new books and project. Then please sign up for my newsletter at www.connorwhiteley.net/

Have a great day.

CHECK OUT THE PSYCHOLOGY WORLD PODCAST FOR MORE PSYCHOLOGY INFORMATION!

AVAILABLE ON ALL MAJOR PODCAST APPS.

About the author:

Connor Whiteley is the author of over 30 books in the sci-fi fantasy, nonfiction psychology and books for writer's genre and he is a Human Branding Speaker and Consultant.

He is a passionate warhammer 40,000 reader, psychology student and author.

Who narrates his own audiobooks and he hosts The Psychology World Podcast.

All whilst studying Psychology at the University of Kent, England.

Also, he was a former Explorer Scout where he gave a speech to the Maltese President in August 2018 and he attended Prince Charles' 70th Birthday Party at Buckingham Palace in May 2018.

Plus, he is a self-confessed coffee lover!

Please follow me on:

Website: www.connorwhiteley.net

Twitter: @scifiwhiteley

Please leave on honest review as this helps with the discoverability of the book and I truly appreciate it.

Thank you for reading. I hope you've enjoyed.

All books in 'An Introductory Series':

BIOLOGICAL PSYCHOLOGY 3RD
EDITION

COGNITIVE PSYCHOLOGY 2ND
EDITION

SOCIAL PSYCHOLOGY- 3RD EDITION

ABNORMAL PSYCHOLOGY 3RD
EDITION

PSYCHOLOGY OF RELATIONSHIPS-
3RD EDITION

DEVELOPMENTAL PSYCHOLOGY 3RD
EDITION

HEALTH PSYCHOLOGY

RESEARCH IN PSYCHOLOGY

A GUIDE TO MENTAL HEALTH AND
TREATMENT AROUND THE WORLD-
A GLOBAL LOOK AT DEPRESSION

FORENSIC PSYCHOLOGY

CLINICAL PSYCHOLOGY

FORMULATION IN PSYCHOTHERAPY

Other books by Connor Whiteley:

THE ANGEL OF RETURN

THE ANGEL OF FREEDOM

GARRO: GALAXY'S END

GARRO: RISE OF THE ORDER

GARRO: END TIMES

GARRO: SHORT STORIES

GARRO: COLLECTION

GARRO: HERESY

GARRO: FAITHLESS

GARRO: DESTROYER OF WORLDS

GARRO: COLLECTIONS BOOK 4-6

GARRO: MISTRESS OF BLOOD

GARRO: BEACON OF HOPE

GARRO: END OF DAYS

WINTER'S COMING

WINTER'S HUNT

WINTER'S REVENGE

WINTER'S DISSENSION

Companion guides:

BIOLOGICAL PSYCHOLOGY 2ND EDITION WORKBOOK

COGNITIVE PSYCHOLOGY 2ND EDITION WORKBOOK

SOCIOCULTURAL PSYCHOLOGY 2ND EDITION WORKBOOK

ABNORMAL PSYCHOLOGY 2ND EDITION WORKBOOK

PSYCHOLOGY OF HUMAN RELATIONSHIPS 2ND EDITION WORKBOOK

HEALTH PSYCHOLOGY WORKBOOK

FORENSIC PSYCHOLOGY WORKBOOK

Audiobooks by Connor Whiteley:

BIOLOGICAL PSYCHOLOGY

COGNITIVE PSYCHOLOGY

SOCIOCULTURAL PSYCHOLOGY

ABNORMAL PSYCHOLOGY

PSYCHOLOGY OF HUMAN RELATIONSHIPS

HEALTH PSYCHOLOGY

DEVELOPMENTAL PSYCHOLOGY

RESEARCH IN PSYCHOLOGY

FORENSIC PSYCHOLOGY

GARRO: GALAXY'S END

GARRO: RISE OF THE ORDER

GARRO: SHORT STORIES

GARRO: END TIMES

GARRO: COLLECTION

GARRO: HERESY

GARRO: FAITHLESS

GARRO: DESTROYER OF WORLDS

GARRO: COLLECTION BOOKS 4-6

GARRO: COLLECTION BOOKS 1-6

Business books:

TIME MANAGEMENT: A GUIDE FOR STUDENTS AND WORKERS

LEADERSHIP: WHAT MAKES A GOOD LEADER? A GUIDE FOR STUDENTS AND WORKERS.

BUSINESS SKILLS: HOW TO SURVIVE THE BUSINESS WORLD? A GUIDE FOR STUDENTS, EMPLOYEES AND EMPLOYERS.

BUSINESS COLLECTION

GET YOUR FREE BOOK AT:
WWW.CONNORWHITELEY.NET